Stolen Lives

By
Gwendolyn Stephens Baker-Alford

This book is dedicated to Mrs. Arie Lee Smith Stephens, my mother, who was a God-fearing Christian woman and an elementary school teacher who always emphasized the importance of a good education.

Speak up for those who cannot speak for themselves, for the rights of all who are destitute. **Proverbs 31:8 (NIV)**

Fact

A 1977 United States Senate Committee Report on Equal Educational Opportunity stated that "In many ways, the school principal is the most important and influential individual in the school. He or she is the person responsible for all activities that occur in and around the school building. It is the principal's leadership that sets the tone of the school, the climate for teaching, the level of professionalism and morale of teachers, and the degree of concern for what students may or may not become. The principal is the main link between the community and the school, and the way he or she performs in this capacity largely determines the attitude of parents and students about the school. If a school is vibrant, innovative, child-centered place, and if it has a reputation for excellence in teaching, if students are performing to the best of their ability, one can almost always point to the principal's leadership as the key to success."

These are some of the main reasons why the absolute best leaders must be put in charge of schools.

Humiliation

Have you ever told such a sad story that immediately upon hearing it, those listening accuse you of lying. You know it happened, but you just go on and let them think you're lying because it's so embarrassing and humiliating that it's just easier to let them think you're lying. When they laugh, you laugh right along with them, but inside, you're crying because you know these things happened, but you're too ashamed for people to know that you have experienced something like this, especially those who love you because you know they will take on this burden and suffer right along with you. Unfortunately, many things that occur in schools fall into this category of stories__ those that are so sad, they're unbelievable. The most unfortunate aspect of this is the fact that these things happen in schools. The purpose of school is for teachers to teach and students to learn. So, how do these sad incidences infiltrate our schools? These occurrences are the result of poor administrative leadership. It is the principal who sets the standards for his or her school.

A case in point involved an incident when I learned from reading the school board's agenda that I had been transferred over the summer to a different school. When I attempted to contact the new principal of my school to get clarity, he/she didn't answer the phone; however someone began to send a text message. The following is the exchange between the two of us. This message came from the principal's personal mobile phone. A colleague told me that it was the principal's cell phone number and that she had spoken with him/her at this number just prior to her giving it to me. She had called him/her when she discovered that her name was listed on the school board's agenda as resigning when in fact she had not. While I wouldn't ordinarily call a principal's personal phone, I did so because during the summer months when schools were closed, it was very difficult to reach principals at schools due to their scheduled meetings and preparations for the upcoming school year.

The Exchange (via text message)

> Sender: Who is this?
>
> My response: Dr. Baker-Alford
>
> Sender: Why did you call me? I don't know you.
>
> My response: Please call whenever you can. Thanks
>
> Sender: No, I don't know you.
>
> My response: I would appreciate the courtesy of a call.
>
> Sender: Negative, Do you know _____ _____?
>
> My response: I am the instructional coach at Monroe High.
>
> Sender: That's who I am.
>
> My response: I'm confused.
>
> Sender: I am _____ _____. I refuse to call you. Leave my number alone.

While I cannot say for certain that this message came from the new principal, I truly believe it came from his personal mobile phone. I was told later that his good friend, the former principal who had initiated these changes in the school was probably the person who sent the text message. I think most people knew that he/she was capable of such an act as this. And because he/she had been removed from the school, he/she was taking others down with him/her.

This is just one example of the many sad things that happen in schools. These kinds of things should never happen in a school. The level of disrespect and disregard for the feelings of others was atrocious and scary. It's difficult to imagine someone having the gall to do something like this while using a device that could be easily traced. While the text messages were completely unprofessional, the fact that the school board operated in this manner was worse. Board members rarely, if ever, questioned transfers or other recommendations made by school administrators. Even though it was stated in our contracts that the school board could transfer and reassign employees, it was absolutely unprofessional and disrespectful to transfer teachers without their having knowledge of it. And most of the actions taken by the school principals were done out of spite to get even with someone. It is very difficult to think about the fact that these kinds of people were put in charge of schools, but they were, and it continues today. How could they think that sensible people would respect them or take them seriously? The good thing about this was that this principal didn't last long at this particular school. His/her character, or lack thereof, was eventually discovered and he/she was given a safe job away from people.

Loss

When a gun is fired, it doesn't always hit its target instantaneously. Sometimes, it takes years for the bullet to hit the mark. This was the case in our county. The bullet that hit our county had been fired decades earlier, but when it finally reached its target, it exploded and brought the city to its knees. The casualties were everybody, especially if you were in anyway in need of an education then you were brought down because our school district had failed to provide such and had been victimized by bad politics, cliques, poor hiring practices, and many other poor decisions. If you needed a job, most of those that paid a decent salary were no more. They had left. There remained some jobs in education and healthcare that mainly required a college degree or specialized training, but for the masses, there were very few left. Those were mainly jobs in restaurants and fast-food. There were some jobs in retail sales, but real-money jobs had basically become non-existent. And there were no prospects of things getting better for the county because of the low functioning school district. Companies just would not come to a city with a poor school district. They would choose neighboring cities instead. As a result, the county became poorer; the people became more desperate, and crime increased.

Life happens so fast that before you know it, your little baby that you loved so at birth that you vowed to protect and provide the best life possible is now in high school and in a gang and on drugs and is barely hanging on. It happens so fast that you can only wonder, "What happened?" It seems now the road to success that you carved out for your child was just a dream. You thought you had it all figured out. My child will get good grades and score high on the SATs, get scholarships, and off to college he will go. But unfortunately, reality sets in and you don't know how to deal with it because you had other plans for your child. You didn't expect your son to end up on the wrong side of the law. You didn't expect your daughter to get pregnant at sixteen. It should not come as a surprise that this is the new normal. It no longer happens to just "poor children;" it happens to all children, especially those who attend poor schools. I have seen it on a regular basis, and it is especially troubling in the case of parents who are teachers and know first-hand everything they need to do, say, and purchase for their children to succeed. They give it their all and their children end up incarcerated or in one form or another depending on the state, and if they fail to educate their children, what about other parents who perhaps don't know how schools and districts operate. They don't stand a chance of educating theirs, and it's an even greater mistake when they leave it to the schools to do so. Poor schools are poor at educating children. That's why so many children who attend them end up in gangs, on drugs, in and out of jail, and worse places, and also depending on their parents for the rest of their lives. The question of how this can happen persists. While there are many factors that can contribute to these outcomes, schooling in particular, can be named as a major culprit, especially poor schools that use their circumstances or even the children they serve as an excuse for low or no academic achievement. They place blame on the helpless saying that their schools are failing because these children will not come to school or that their parents do not care whether their children get an education. This is an easy answer and a quick fix to place the blame on others, but in actuality, the blame should be placed on those in charge of the schools as well. School leaders should not place all the blame on children and their parents. They are guilty as well. I would say even more so. It is their responsibility to get the parents involved and get the children in the schools. Parents have a tremendous responsibility as well and when they refuse to adhere to the state guidelines such as making sure their children attend school, they should be promptly referred to local law enforcement and dealt with per the state's compulsory attendance laws. Left unchecked, parents contribute to poor schools when they fail in their duties and responsibilities as parents. However, regardless of the circumstances, it is the principal's responsibility to get the parents involved. The principal should never be let off the hook when it comes to parental involvement. He or she has to get it done, whether it is done gingerly or roughly, it has to be done. It is non-negotiable. One might ask the question of how principals can force the hands of parents. The simple answer is that they can turn them in to local authorities for truancy and contact child protective services when children fail to attend school or when students are educationally neglected. The problem with most principals is their reluctance due to fear of being seen as too controversial. However, it is their duty to do so, and if they don't have the guts to take action to make things better for their students, then, they should be removed.

Some things that happen in some school districts are unethical, unlawful, unconscionable, and just plain wrong. I swell when I think of all the politics, improprieties, and misdeeds that occur in some school districts. Leaders are chosen on the basis of their popularity in the system. A person with no classroom experience or educational background might be handed the job of superintendent by the former superintendent as he leaves the district simply because they are buddies, and the school board approves. A school principal with no experience might be hired over someone who has much more experience because he is somebody's son, nephew, frat brother, or friend. Large sums of money are unaccounted for and no one is held accountable. Principals are allowed to remain in schools year after year no matter how low their test scores. People are allowed to attend athletic events without paying entrance fees, thus robbing the schools of resources. People sell things in the name of the school and under the disguise of supporting the school financially, but keep the proceeds. These things continue to happen in schools all over America. There seems to be no end to them and no way to address or fight them in some districts where all the players have some kind of allegiance to each other, and you lose before you even get started. Even though I have left public education, these things continue to tap dance in my head. The only thing that will relieve me from this nightmare is to write about them and expose these practices to the world. Enough is enough.

I will begin with the day-to-day operations of the school during the time I spent as a teacher. I spent many years working in different kinds of schools. Some functioned better than others, but I will focus on those that I feel really hindered academic achievement. My reflections begin in the present tense to create in my readers a feeling of actually being there, or in other words, to make my experiences real for them.

Today, there's a police car parked in front of the school. Yesterday, two police officers had to wrestle an angry parent to the ground and handcuff him. If I stand here long enough, I'll see the cops taking a handcuffed student to their cruiser. What I will not see will be others standing around trying to see what is going on. I will not see the handcuffed student resisting either. The police, arrests, and conflict were common sights at one school where I worked. No one got excited about such things. Students did not resist; they knew the routine very well. Neither did they resist other life-threatening acts like gang banging, robbing, stealing, drug-dealing, and killing. They did it all. Unfortunately, because they had seen it all. Most of them had been robbed of childhood, and the only things left to them were the streets that stole their childhood and forced them to become men and women far too soon. And unfortunately, this was where many learned what they thought was survival. If I had to paint a picture of their lives, it would be a collection of their life experiences __ those that you see in the streets like shootings and killings, homelessness, and the constant and persistent sight of the drug dealer cruising the neighborhood. This was their montage, a collection of life experiences that robbed these children of their childhood. In other words, their lives were stolen.

When you are a caring teacher working in a school of poor children, you have something to cry about every day. I began my teaching career in the late seventies in an affluent predominately white school district. There was never anything to cry about. My crying started many years later when I began teaching in a school district where the majority of students were poor blacks. Some lived in deplorable environments, and the circumstances of their personal lives were as bad if not worse. So that was when I started crying. This book is the story of my journey through a place called school, the people I met on the way, and how we cried and tried but failed our students anyway, in my opinion because there was a mountain of obstacles before us, most of which we accepted and allowed by failing to speak out and make a real attempt to address the improprieties and politics in our school district. During the years I worked as a teacher, I worked in several districts, so while this book covers my experiences in some of them, it mainly reflects my experiences in one in particular.

I suppose in all our lives, as children, we do not concern ourselves with adult matters. We go about our way innocently never realizing that some experiences will be with us the rest of our lives. I had such an experience as a child, but it took many years to realize what that experience would cost me. In the early years of my life, my family, like most in those days, didn't have a lot. Our lives consisted of going to church, school, and to work when there was work. But there was wealth in being able to dream of having better and living better. We were loaded when it came to dreaming. My dream was to be a ballerina. I lived this dream constantly. Every day, when school would dismiss, I would rush to the library and check out books about famous ballerinas and performances. These things were magical to me. Nothing seemed more beautiful than the ladies outfitted in their beautiful tutus standing on their toes with a back drop of some beautiful place like nothing I had ever seen living in the country and being surrounded by livestock and acres of bare fields. I felt that was my calling because I absolutely loved it, but as a child, I did not know that something like that was not possible for me given our circumstances. For some reason, I just believed that I could have it even though there was nothing in sight that suggested I could.

As impossible as it had seemed, one day, the opportunity presented itself.

It happened when I was in fourth grade. I recall sitting in my classroom with my classmates while my teacher was away. The teacher's absence created a dilemma for me because I had to go to the restroom but was afraid to go without asking her. But it came to the point where I had to go and so I did. I hurried o the restroom, used it, washed my hands, and walked back to the classroom all the while hoping my teacher had not gotten back to the room. As I walked, I heard a beautiful melody that got my attention. I crept over to peep into the room where the sound was coming from. It was then that I saw my teacher and a couple of others directing some of my classmates in a Hawaiian dance. These girls were outfitted in beautiful grass skirts and leis, and flowers adorned their heads. They waved their arms gracefully from side to side and moved so that their grass skirts seemed to shimmer when they met the sunlight coming through the classroom window. All I could see was a beautiful sight___ an opportunity to finally get to dance __the one thing I wanted the most. For me, it meant being the ballerina I always wanted to be. But then I realized that I was not in the room with the other girls. I was standing outside peeping in at them. In fact, I would never have known anything about them had I not just happen to hear the song. In other words, I had not been invited to be a part of it. And as a child, I was too afraid to ask, but in actuality, I think that I didn't ask because I knew they didn't want me. I was also smart enough to know why. I was not like the girls in the room. All of them were light-complexioned with long thick ropy hair. Their hair was what people called "good hair" in those days. So as I walked back to the classroom, I hung my head with the realization that even black people discriminate against black people. My own people who I had considered a safe haven, had their prejudices too. They judged me by my looks and not by my talent and wit. I had been naïve, but this experience made me realize that just because you are a black student with black teachers that doesn't mean that you are not going to experience discrimination and humiliation. This was the same school I was attending when Dr. King was killed. While Dr. King and others were out there paying the ultimate price to make a difference in the lives of black people and creating in us a sense of pride in our heritage and ancestors, our own people were telling us that we were not white enough to be included or taken seriously. This experience created in me a feeling of inferiority. It made me feel like I was not as good as some others. I likened it to one of the determining factors in the Brown vs Board of Education decision that concluded that separating children on the basis of race creates a dangerous inferiority complex that may adversely affect black children's ability to learn. This experience also created in me a desire to be honest about how black teachers hurt black students. As African Americans, we are quick to point out the systemic racism of white America, but slow to admit to our own practices of separation and discrimination. When I was not allowed to be a part of the dance team, I was separated from the others. Because my skin was darker than theirs and my hair was not long, I experienced discrimination. They didn't want me. They didn't open the doors of participation for girls who looked like me.

I realized as I got older that my opinion about these kinds of things was an unpopular one and would cause me a great deal of pain because every black person who ever blamed black people for their own failures and oversights has been called a sell-out regardless of whether he or she was being honest, but I want allow fear of ridicule to stop me from telling this story. There's something more pressing and important than my feelings, and that thing is black-on-black suppression and discrimination. These things are real, and unfortunately, there exist no proper channels to address them. Most governmental agencies like the EEOC and the ACLU that address discrimination on so many levels have nothing in place to address black- on-black suppression and discrimination, and this is probably due to the fact that society doesn't feel that black people discriminate against blacks. I attribute this lack of awareness of black discrimination to the many acts of crime committed by blacks against blacks such as black-on-black murder, domesticate abuse, and job discrimination. The more it is ignored, the worse the problem will get. Whether they are governmental agencies, the court and penal system, or schools, they have all failed to address black-on-black discrimination, and unfortunately this lack of attention has caused some black people to devalue their own people. This failure manifests in the form of blacks shooting and killing other blacks like it is nothing. And the thing that is almost as tragic as the killings themselves is that we use generational poverty as the reason for these kinds of things, and we always blame generational poverty on slavery. But the truth is, none of us were ever slaves. Our forefathers and mothers were, but we were not slaves. We are the descendants of slaves, but we were not slaves; I do, however, recognize the fact that our lives are adversely impacted by the institution of slavery and systemic racism, but we cannot allow that fact to stop us in our tracks. We must demand more, fight harder and persevere. We cannot continue to fail to educate our children and use slavery and poverty as reasons why we cannot progress. I cannot emphasize enough that slavery was real for those who lived it, but not for us, not in the same way it was for them. That is why it is so easy for some blacks to say things like," I wish I were around back then, I wouldn't have taken that." One cannot speak about circumstances that he has not experienced. I believe that if slaves were around today, they would laugh at us. For all their suffering, exploitation, and their dreams of a better time and place, how have we honored them: fatherless families, teenage pregnancies, song lyrics that constantly and consistently set out to debase and destroy the black woman by renaming her "bitch." And unfortunately, many black females, instead of fighting the madness have become willing participants in it and refer to themselves as "bitch." They use it as a term of endearment. "I am that bitch."

My journey begins in an old building once used to teach educators how to deliver instructions. But instead, we learned not to say anything, never to complain, to sit and listen, and follow orders. Many years later, I find myself here again, but I am not here to learn anything. I'm here to trick someone into giving me what I need because the powers that be probably will not let me get it the honest way, so I'm going to have to strategize and maneuver to take it from them without them knowing it. As I creep down the halls that I walked so many times before, I do so with a sense of dread and fear because there are probably still some very vicious people in the building, and if they do not like you, they will go out of their way to make things difficult for you. Sadly, these kinds of people were the ones in charge, and they could make things difficult for you because most were in cliques with other school leaders and they always presented a united front whenever they felt threatened by outsiders, those who were not in their circle. They did it because it worked. Many, out of fear, would never go up against them. They would just go ahead and accept the situation to avoid getting on the bad side of the wrong people. Those who didn't, suffered.

There were many forms of abuse. Some happened at the central office, and some occurred in the individual schools. For example, out of spite and to humiliate a persistent teacher, the principal might ask a teacher to pass a student who had not done anything the entire year, or a teacher might be asked to change a student's grade to make him or her eligible for honor roll, and when it came to athletes, a teacher might be asked to do anything. To refuse to do these things always made matters worse for the teacher. A standoff would ensue; teacher versus principal, and the outcome would be the teacher would lose to the principal and his domination and control would get worse being that winning has validated him and now he is hydrated, fortified, and ready for round two, and the teacher becomes his dog. Unfortunately, I find myself here again in this awful place called school. Actually, it had been converted to a teachers' resource facility. I have business that puts me in the crosshairs of anyone who never got a chance to get me while I was in the district and has since waited patiently for their opportunity. Perhaps, this sounds paranoid, but it isn't actually. If I am paranoid, I am not alone. There are countless other individuals who experienced these kinds of things.

It is sad that as I walk through these halls, the only thing I can really feel is fear and a dread that someone is going to try to make it hard for me to get what I need. As I continue through these halls, I think back on all the lives that were impacted by what the school system had an opportunity to do but failed to do. I think back on all the lives that were altered, and in some cases, ruined by what went on in this building. Here, it was that my colleagues and I received many lessons on classroom concepts that were supposed to sharpen our intellectual skills as teachers. To be able to reminisce should be a pleasant experience, but today's experience is everything but pleasant. Instead, I enter the hallway with an expectation of trouble. A gloom pervades the air and a warning emanates from the walls,

"Go back." I can't turn around, though, because I have business of importance that I must attend to.

As I navigate the long halls in search of my destination, I dare not stop and ask for directions. I will not take a chance on being recognized. Each hall displays an announcement. Most of them announced some kind of teacher workshop. As I read each, I am reminded of the many I sat through during my tenure as a teacher in the district. They brought back memories of the way things were in the system: the politics and the buddy system where friends hired friends and people in their cliques. The walls made me think about the countless workshops where teachers were expected to listen in silence, acquiesce, and accept misinformation regardless of the extent of misrepresentation and irrelevance. Teachers were expected to be on board with the most ridiculously counterproductive procedures or what higher-ups called "policy" or "mandates" when they wanted to frighten teachers into compliance. While lacking in intelligence and common sense, most of these so-called school leaders were experts in their use of operative terms. Words such as "downtown" meaning the "central office," "the state", "the superintendent", "insubordination", were their triggers to get the job done. At the end of the day, the joke, however, was on them. While most teachers gave them a nod to say they were on board, many of them, as soon as they returned to their schools, closed their doors and did what they thought they needed to do in their classrooms. In order to keep their jobs, these teachers put on a façade of cooperation in the face of what many of them considered to be ignorant and overbearing school leaders who were misguided and worked under the duress of the good old boy network that gave the orders about what would and would not happen in the district and who would be promoted and who would not. In spite of all the politics, dishonesty, and injustices, there were those teachers who did what they had to do to help their students; however, this was not always the best thing either. It was just better than the alternative. For every teacher who did what she or he thought was necessary, there were two or three who closed their doors and did nothing except pacify their students with worksheets. In essence, had there been meaningful training and school leaders who really cared, things would have probably been better across the board, but outrageous policies and politics only contributed to apathy and resentment and destroyed morale and enthusiasm among teachers.

    We were almost always screaming for some kind of attention to our problems in the district, but most of them went ignored, so it got to the place where teachers stopped trying and just accepted things the way they were. The leaders would ignore us in departmental, faculty, and district meetings; yet, they expected us to take them seriously: to listen to them and heed their directives. How could we, though, when they ignored our cries for help? It took me a while to realize that perhaps some of them could not help us. After all, just because someone was put in charge, that didn't necessarily mean that he/she was capable of doing that job. Some of them would even come out and just tell us that they didn't know why they were selected for a particular job. They would have applied for them and gotten them, but we knew how they had gotten them, and they knew as well. The thing that puzzled me was why they would tell us that they didn't feel qualified. Perhaps, feelings of guilt made them confess. Their confessions, however, didn't do a lot to build our confidence in them. I don't know what they expected to get out of it, but it was as if they were telling us that they couldn't help us and not to expect them to be of benefit. The thing they missed was that they were talking to intelligent human beings who expected them to be able to solve problems and make things better. After all, they expected us to be onboard with whatever they instructed us to do. Perhaps, if we had been programmed robots, we could have done this, but how can one expect intelligent and sensitive people to accept this without feeling a certain amount of resentment and frustration. It was as if they were suggesting we ignore our feelings, suppress them, and deny that we even had feelings. Their expectations were unrealistic and created low morale in the district, but they didn't seem to care.

Now, back to my reason for being in this building today. I have school business of a personal nature that involves a former student. I am going to get his high school transcript and apply for the diploma that he should have gotten many years ago. This student, like thousands of others in the state, had been denied his because he failed a state-required graduation test. Even though he had a high GPA and had passed all of the tests except one, he was still denied his diploma. This had been a terrible injustice to students because the state ignored all of their other accomplishments and punished them on the basis of one failure. Recently, however, the state mandated that any student who was denied his diploma because of the state –required graduation tests could now get his. So today, I am attempting to complete the first step in the process and that is to get his transcript. But, I have this nagging fear that I won't be able to get it because of who I am.

I was disliked by many people in the school system because I would speak out against incompetence, unethical hiring practices, and retaliatory administrators. I was not shy about expressing my opinion, and this made me a very unpopular person in the system, and that's putting it mildly. The truth of the matter is that I was often targeted, subjected to all sorts of retaliatory actions, and generally singled out and harassed. And I say generally because it happened so often. It was my new normal, and I hated it. As a matter-of-fact, one of my greatest joys in teaching *Beowulf* was to picture myself as the monster Grendel prowling the hall and ravaging my tormentors one at a time. I wanted to devour them. Lol!

While my tenure in the school district was marked by many instances of harassment and retaliation, there were others that offset all the negativity, and they were my experiences at Albany State University, Valdosta State University, Georgia Southwestern State University, and Florida A&M University. During the time I worked on my Ph.D. at FAMU, I was recognized and awarded for my contributions to their Educational Leadership Program. Among my accomplishments, I was assigned membership into the Golden Key International Honour Society. My time at FAMU and the other universities were encouraging and kept my self-worth intact. This was especially important to me because the school district had all but destroyed my self-confidence. I had to be really strong to hold on to my self-worth, and my advice to others caught in such a struggle is to seek out those people and institutions that promote growth. Don't let the negativity and those with an agenda destroy you and make you feel like you are not capable. The problem is generally with them and not you, and if you don't go along just to get along, they have no use for you.

I am now retired and have been for a while, but there's always the possibility of someone recognizing me as I make my way to the records office. So, today, as I meander through the building, I am hoping that I will not be recognized, for surely if I am, there's always the possibility of someone denying my request simply because of who I am. This was quite common in the system. A person was either supported or condemned depending on what others thought of him or her. If you were a good old boy or girl who went with the status quo, then you were supported. On the other hand, if you did the opposite, then you were ostracized, denied, and suffered retaliation. And this was done with total disregard for civil rights and federal laws prohibiting discriminatory practices in the workplace. To those in charge, there was nothing to fear about a discrimination lawsuit because the district almost always prevailed. The thought of a potential federal lawsuit against the system was a joke. Being right and having a good case counted for nothing. If you were disliked, you were scorned and there was nothing you could do about your situation because most of these perpetrators of injustice were heads of major offices and they all ran in the same circles. If one disliked you, they all did, and it was as if they took pleasure in seeing you suffer. They would send you on a wild-goose chase from office to office trying to clear the simplest of matters. All the while, they would be calling each other and sharing laughs and planning in advance how they were going to handle you once you got to their offices. One of the worst of these characters was a person who worked at the central office. This person was very unprofessional, and seemed to have been out of control. There was an occasion when I went in to see the superintendent. After about an hour of meeting with him, I got up to leave. When I opened his door to leave, this person almost fell into his office. I didn't say anything and neither did the other person who witnessed this, but I believe the superintendent saw her because she was eventually removed from the central office.

As I approach the window to the records office, I see that there's a figure that I do not recognize, and since I don't know her she probably doesn't know me. This is good. Now, I can breathe a sigh of relief. As I state my business, she hands me papers and asks me to sign them. I read them quickly and sign them smiling all the while. This seems to calm her, and now the rest should be easy. For some strange reason, smiling faces made these people act a little better, so regardless of how you felt inside, you had to smile to keep them from blocking you. I resented having to smile at any of them because I knew what they were after. A smile meant that you were on board with the system. You were a friend. Being a friend to such a misguided group of people was the very last thing on my mind. I could not have resented them more. So, I put on my clown face to get something I needed. Now, back to the task at hand. After I am done signing these, she explains what will happen next. She explains that these will be sent to the next level for review and approval. I was not quite over the hurdle yet, though, because the next level was headed by a person who I once reported to the superintendent for publishing low test scores for our school when in fact we had high test scores in some areas. This person had reported our school's test scores as the lowest in the system and in the school board minutes which was an official public document. I felt this was wrong. Our students had worked extremely hard, and they deserved to be recognized. They certainly did not deserve to be thought of as having the lowest scores in the system. At the time, no one else would say anything for fear of retaliation, but I felt compelled to say something. I had worked directly with the students and knew how hard they had worked. Had I not said anything, these students would have had to bear the burden of being labeled the lowest in the district when they were actually one of the higher scoring schools.

As I expected, when school opened the next year, I paid for my gall. I had been demoted over the summer. My demotion was the message to others that you better keep your mouth shut. If I had to do it all over again, I would. Our school was predominantly black and served many poor children. It was one of few schools that had managed to remain open under mandatory desegregation. Most black high schools became junior high schools during that era, but this school survived as a high school. And this was not what some of the locals wanted, so at every turn, the school was a target. Whenever crimes were committed in the city, the perpetrator would be connected to our school if he or she had ever been a student there or was currently attending our school. When test scores were publicized, our school would always be listed at the bottom. When explanations were given as to why the system's SAT scores were low, old file footage of our school would be shown on the local news. When our school did well, there were either misleading reports or none at all. I am not saying that we always had high scores, but there were times when our scores would be high in certain subject areas. In other words, there seemed to be an effort put forth to highlight our failures and ignore our successes.

As far as today's visit, the process went smoothly overall, and at the end of it, I was told that the diploma would arrive in approximately two weeks. However, I attribute this to the fact that I did not have to see the person at "the next level," the person that I had turned in for reporting inaccurate test scores for our school. Perhaps she was out that day. I saw the assistant instead, a former student of mine who had a great deal of respect for me as a classroom teacher and knew and accepted my no-nonsense policies. I knew her well and remembered her to be a student who was honest and highly intelligent. She did not belong to that aforementioned class of individuals, and in playing it straight with me, she was not showing me favoritism; she was just doing her job. I always took special notice of those who performed their jobs as professionals. I never took them for granted because ethics and fairness were rare practices in our system.

The diploma arrived in about two weeks as I had been told and this meant that there was one less student in the state without a high-school diploma, but there were thousands more (for one reason or another) who would not get theirs, not to mention the millions in future generations who are already doomed if the drop-out rate continues as it is today. When I think about the millions of children who are trapped in poor schools, I feel compelled to tell their story. As a classroom teacher who always really cared, I cannot ignore the poison that has infiltrated our schools and robbed children of their education and stolen their lives.

The story of these children's lives is a sad one, and the unique circumstances of their individual lives can be compared to an image I once saw that was so disturbing that I have been unable to block it from my memory and am not sure that I want to block it out because it is a reminder of how poorly run schools victimize their students and leave them to pick up the pieces of their lives. So, I choose to let it torment me whenever I think about it because I deserve to be tormented and everybody else who stands idly by and allow this to happen, educators in particular. We all deserve to be tormented for knowing the problems of poor schools and ignoring them, or worse, covering them up to protect our own salaries when children all around us are dying the slow death of ignorance which will eventually manifest itself in the form of poverty and criminal acts to lessen the impact of it all.

The image I saw was that of a skinny, emaciated, and pitiful looking arm reaching desperately through a tiny hole of an old bent and rusty steal door of a jail cell. The arm was stretched as far as possible through this tiny hole to where the underarm on the other side of the door was probably right up against the door. No other part of this person could be seen, just his arm. The arm was desperate in its reach and seemed to beg for something beyond my ability to imagine. There was a desperation in its reach that tormented me. The thought that this child was probably incarcerated for a good reason was oblivious to me because the image of his little skinny arm made me feel so badly that I couldn't care what he had done. The only thing I could feel for this child was pity. I felt sorry that the little arm seemed so desperate and pitiful. I felt sorry that he seemed so young, alone and abandoned. I was tormented by the fact that I couldn't figure out what he might have been reaching for. All kinds of thoughts came to my mind. I thought about who his mother was and where she was, and how she could bear seeing her child like this. And then I imagined his situation being so much like those of other children like him who were raised without fathers in their homes, those children who grow up in dilapidated and blighted neighborhoods where the sight of drug dealers, prostitution, and homelessness comprise the landscape, despair is common, and hope does not exist. I just wanted this child's mama to come and get him. Like most people would have, I guess I was naturally inclined to want this child to have a mama somewhere whose motherly instincts made her care more than anyone else and would do anything to get her child out of this situation, but then reality set in and made me realize that there might not be a mama.

I will never know exactly why this child ended up here. I cannot place the blame on his upbringing; the only thing I can do is suspect that it had something to do with his situation. I can, however, attribute some of his condition to poor schooling because I have seen first-hand the devastating impact poor schools have on the lives of children, especially children like this young desperate child reaching out through a jail cell. Many children like him have reached out for a lifeline only to have it thrown back at them. Poor schools steal lives, and perhaps they had stolen this child's life. He could have been anybody's child including mine or yours, but I will refer to him as "My Child" because, as teachers, we are the parents of these children when they are in our care. We should care about every aspect of their lives.

When I retired, I thought it would be a time for relaxation and forgetting all the things I had experienced in the schools. It was quite the opposite. I could not relax because I was tormented by the things I knew about the schools. There were too many wrongs, too many secrets, too much injustice, and too much politics. Just knowing this and remembering what we had gone through in the system and the fact that these things were concealed would not allow me to rest and relax. My peace was held hostage, and I realized the only way to freedom was to tear down the walls that concealed and protected those who did not care and whose actions corrupted the system and cheated students out of an education; those who harassed good teachers and caused them to lose their jobs; those who got their big salaries and could not care less about the poor children who depended on them to help make their lives at least tolerable.

Most educators know the Latin term "in loco parentis" meaning "in the place of a parent." Anyone who has ever studied education knows that "in loco parentis" is a legal doctrine describing a relationship similar to that of a parent to a child. It refers to an individual who assumes parental status and responsibilities for another individual. If more educators in the system had practiced "in loco parentis," fewer children would have died the slow death of ignorance, apathy, and lack of discipline and love, but unfortunately, in many of these schools, these children lost their lives.

Many students experienced a holocaust, a systemic pattern of destruction, and not all of the blame could be placed on the teachers and administrators. Some of these children were their own worst enemies. They victimized themselves with their lack of respect for their teachers, their attitudes toward school in general: their baseless accusations against teachers, cutting class, fighting, and making teaching and learning impossible. But the most unfortunate thing of all was that very few educators seemed to care enough to stop the madness. Perhaps, they felt as I did. I could not sympathize with them because, as a child, I experienced many trials and tribulations but studied hard and succeeded in spite of the circumstances. My childhood like many of the children I grew up with had been affected by poverty. Meals were not routine for people in those days. They were a blessing, and people didn't take them for granted but were motivated to stay the course. There were days when people ate and days when they wanted to eat. No one lamented the hungry days; they accepted them. Getting an education was not easy either. There were many things that stood in our way. For example, when we could not make it to the bus stop on time and would see the bus driver driving off in spite of seeing us running as fast as the wind blows, we did not stop running. We kept running until we got to school. When we got there, there would be only about three hours left in the school day because of the distance between our houses and the school. And even though we did not have a lot, we didn't let that stop us from doing the best we could. Our manner and conduct were like that of the rich thanks to my mother who made sure we grew up with a global perspective of the world. We practiced and studied religion with missionaries. We listened to all kinds of music, especially classical music. We joined music clubs via magazines, and it was fine with my mother as long as we purchased some classical music. It couldn't be all Motown. It had to be Beethoven, Chopin, and Vivaldi as well. We listened to and learned the song lyrics of singers like Sammy Davis Jr, Dean Martin, Frank Sinatra, Johnnie Mathis, and Sam Cooke. In fact, Sam Cooke was my first crush. I fell in love with the man's music and then with him. "Cupid" was my favorite. I would stare into his face on the album cover, sway from side to side, and sing right along with him, "Cupid, draw back your bow and let your arrow go straight to my lover's heart for me, for me." And then one day, my mother told me that he was dead. I thought to myself, "lucky me; I've fallen in love with a dead man; someone I would never see." I doubt if I would have ever seen him anyway even if he hadn't been dead. This was such a terrible blow to me, though, because I was absolutely in love with the man. I learned that he had died long before I was old enough to know what a crush was.

My mother was a dedicated educator, and I learned a great deal about teaching from the things she taught me and the experiences she provided for me. My mother's teaching career began in Roberta,

Georgia, but the majority of her career was spent in Ellaville Georgia. I recall sitting in her classroom as a little girl during the week of pre-planning. I would assist her in getting her classroom ready for the school year. I would use stencils to cut out letters for her bulletin boards, dust off shelves, fill them with books, hang posters, and organize school materials and supplies for students.

I recall going to Mr. Robert Aaron's funeral with my mother. He was the principal of the school where she worked when he passed away. Many years later, his son became superintendent of Terrell County schools. I remember the church being packed with people. My mother introduced me to some of her co-workers. All of them were nice and seemed to be so enthusiastic. They were all very beautiful people and classy, and they seemed so caring. My mother's colleagues left an impression on me, and I recall thinking how nice it must be to be a teacher.

My mother was also civic-minded and involved herself in community affairs. Whenever something needed to be done, she would take the task upon herself with or without assistance from others. She was not one who would wait on others to do what needed to be done. In my hometown of Americus, Georgia, there were many things that warranted attention and that would improve the status and conditions of black neighborhoods. One of these things, in particular, was some of the street names in black neighborhoods such as those that were called "alleys" instead of streets, drives, avenues, etc. My mother had strong feelings about these kinds of things and sought to improve this. She petitioned the city and was instrumental in bringing about a change in names from "alleys" to more proper and fitting names. For example, "Peppermint Alley" became "Peppermint Way."

My dream of becoming a dancer was not totally lost. After my mother finished college and became a teacher, dancing became a reality for me. I didn't become a ballerina, but I performed modern dance with my mother's dance team at her school. In knowing how much dancing meant to me, my mother engaged me as often as possible. When she was attending Albany State College, she would oftentimes catch a glimpse of some rehearsals of the modern dance team there and would tell me what she had seen. I would listen intently and be mesmerized. My mother fed our creative energies in every possible way. Her desire was for us to have a global view of the world, and not be inhibited or limited by our economic condition. Her efforts paid off. Seven of my parents 'eight children went to college. Four of the seven finished, and two are Ph.D.'s. I feel that it is very important for parents to provide all kinds of positive educational and cultural experiences for their children. While lack of resources might pose a problem, parents must learn to be creative to accomplish the goal of providing positive experiences. These experiences will make a difference in a child's future.

While there are many reasons for my book, one main reason is to call attention to the conditions in some schools that lead children (mostly African Americans) into such desperate situations as "My Child." This young man had been victimized by a system that disregarded him, and he was victimized again by a penal system that punished him for conditions for which he had no control. At his young age, what could he have done to have ended up in a place like this?

Having spent thirty plus years teaching in different schools and systems, this is something I know to be true. Many of our former students are the ones who are locked up in these jails and find themselves in hopeless situations because, in part, their schools failed them. For the many years that I taught, I saw students come tattered and torn, angry, resentful, disruptive, doubtful, and troubled, but attending for some reason. Some were there for the meals, and many were not old enough to quit so they were just buying time. However, as a teacher, I did not have time to stop and think about why they were there. My job was to teach them and not judge them. And so teaching was what I did.

I would be lying to say that I did not wish for better students. I wished for those students naturally motivated and well-behaved, but I didn't have them; I had to teach regardless. Unfortunately, some teachers could not accept these conditions and they adopted the attitude that nothing they could do would put a dent in conditions like these, so they didn't do anything except go through the motion, and like the children, they bought their time. They attended faculty meetings and training sessions but many never voiced concerns. It was as if they saw the situation as hopeless, so complaining wouldn't make things better. Some went back to school and got advanced degrees, but these things were done more to increase their salaries and advance their careers than to learn how to help poor children who desperately needed a way out.

Many of these students had no control over their situations. Most of them were living in survival mode without any means of survival. I guess it is sad but factual to say that many were just existing. They were just there, breathing the air. The tragic thing about poverty is that it can be so debilitating and destructive that it seems to paralyze its victims to the point that they are incapable of discerning the dire situation in which they live. In other words, there are no why's or how's in their lives. For them, especially young children, they don't hope for a time when things will be better for them, or a place where circumstances are different, or a reason why, or a way out. They just accept their condition. Perhaps, this is because they know no other. This is where education matters the most. Those who are educated and charged with educating children, are supposed to create that bit of hope. Their job is to motivate the hopeless. Unfortunately, many educators blamed these conditions on the families themselves, but the children in our schools were powerless and rendered virtually helpless. They came to us, and many of us failed them. For many of them, school was an experience that was a waste of their time. Some are no better off today than they were when they first walked through our doors. The blame here can be placed squarely on the shoulders of many of the teachers and school administrators who should have cared enough to really help these children. I had to write this book for them because they were robbed and, the problem persists today. A lot of people would like to think that schools are better now. Unfortunately, this is not the case. Students continue to be victimized by systems run by people who have established an agenda of politics, greed, and corruption, all that comprise the "good old boy/girl" network. Again, I'm writing this book because I cannot, in good conscience, sit back and hide what I know: that poor teaching, the buddy system, corruption, and politics have robbed children of opportunity and hope.

This is the story of my journey through a vicious cycle of what was supposed to be school, a place that educates children and gives them a fair chance at life, but neglected opportunity instead. An even worse tragedy is the fact that those who created these conditions in our schools were mostly blacks working with poor black children. They were the ones in charge and could have made a real difference, but they chose to put themselves first and leave the scraps for the hopeless and the helpless. I know that I will probably get a lot of backlash from some blacks who will say that I'm a sell-out for writing this, and I offer no apology for this and I never will because it is the truth, and what some of them did was unconscionable and will impact some of these students the rest of their lives. My question for those who take offense is, "Wouldn't you want better for your child?" This book is not a representation or a generalization about black people. Rather, it is about what some blacks did in our schools. In contrast, there were many well-meaning black teachers and administrators who worked diligently to provide for the students, and this book is written for them as well. It is a salute to those educators who did all they could under the circumstances like Ms. Patricia Jackson, an educator who never turned down an opportunity to help someone else and who taught her students how to survive in the world by becoming entrepreneurs, and Mr. Robert Simmons, the no – nonsense assistant principal who understood the importance of discipline in the school and recognized that discipline enables teachers to teach and students to learn, so he did his job. Mr. Simmons would also visit English classes and recite "Invictus" so beautifully that it was inspiring. Anyone who has ever heard him can attest to this. The math teacher, Mr. Rufus Phillips, would take students on many field trips to visit colleges to expose them to college life as a way of motivating them to attend themselves, and Ms. Delores Spears, who was one of our principals was caring and a good person as well as a good principal. She conducted faculty meetings like prayer meetings. There were times when it was difficult to tell whether she was praying or conducting a meeting. Her success had to do with the fact that she was humble and respectful of others, and she genuinely cared about the students. She fought for them, and cried for them as well. I was always so proud of Ms. Shirley Brown who was a physical education teacher, athletic director and curriculum person because she would never compromise the school's policies for anyone or anything, and this was rare because some people who held positions like hers would do anything to keep those jobs. Mr. William Thomas, social studies teacher was everything a teacher should be, and Ms. Janice Mikes was a very good English teacher who transformed her classroom into another planet to keep her lessons interesting and to entertain her students. Mr. Charles Price was a visionary in the district. He created internship and job opportunities for students by allowing them to work as stylists, barbers, and entrepreneurs in his place of business. This list can go on continuously because I was at this school for more than two decades and met many smart, dedicated, and hard-working people. And the most inspiring and beloved person in our school was Ms. Juanita Anderson who was also known as Ms. Green and Gold (the school's colors) because she was so dedicated to the success of the school, and her support of the school was unwavering.

A great number of teachers and administrators worked in dire conditions. In many instances, the cards were stacked against them, and they were singled out and humiliated at every turn. They had to be mindful of their thoughts and dare not speak them aloud, especially if they were in any way sensible and logical. It was as if the system frowned on the logical and hated it even more. These educators had to measure each step and tread lightly because they knew what they were up against. The bottom line was that the system perpetrated a regime of fear to control those they considered to be the enemy. But these people were not enemies to the system. They had simply endured too many wrongs, tolerated too much favoritism, and suffered too much retaliation and disrespect. They were overwhelmed.

Many teachers retired, resigned, moved to other systems, or left education altogether to pursue other careers. I cannot emphasize enough the importance of this book for them. They were the ones who really cared, but were not supported. Some could no longer tolerate the conditions.

I hold a deep reverence for the educators who really cared. This book is written with them in mind. It is written to free their minds and consciences and to produce in them a feeling of relief that their story has finally been told as well. I feel fairly certain that even though many of them have moved on with their lives, many still harbor a lingering desire for closure. Because these situations were so suppressive and humiliating, I am sure many long for some kind of relief that will permit them closure. To be at peace, the soul must have closure. I hope this book will finally give them that closure.

When I began writing this book, I tried to tell this story without calling attention to the worst incidences, but I was constantly haunted by the fact that secrecy and denial were the reasons some of the district's schools failed in the first place. Failure to disclose wrongdoing in an effort to protect buddies was what caused these conditions and ultimately caused schools to fail our students, so I came to the conclusion that I have no choice but to present the situations and people as they were. In essence, this book tells the truth, something that is often distorted in some districts. It also lays out the realities of many schools. It provides a clear picture of what children are up against and, in some instances, what parents can do to help their own children rather than expecting the schools to do what most either won't do or cannot do because of the conditions. Some information might appear to be contradictory, and it is because it accurately reflects the schools themselves which were full of contradictions and inconsistencies.

I will begin with discipline. Lack of discipline and chaotic environments are major obstacles to the overall success of any school. I am starting here because discipline is a fundamental value that is so often taken for granted or ignored in most schools. Far too many administrators either do not have the tenacity to deal with disciplinary issues, or they are afraid that following policy will cost them their jobs. To follow policy, in some cases, was to defy the directives of board members, and no one wanted to be accused of that. There would be school board members who would pressure school administrators into compromising the schools' policies. Out of fear, many would take the bait and go along just to keep their jobs. Those who did not would spend the remainder of the school year looking over their shoulders and dreading the renewal and transfer lists for the upcoming school year. They knew they had a big red bullseye on their backs.

Ignoring the school's discipline policies was common depending on the circumstances and the people involved. A case in point: Cell phones had been determined by school leaders to be a detriment and distraction for students and therefore forbidden by the school board which had outlined and mandated procedures for dealing with students caught using cell phones during school hours. Board policy was that teachers and administrators confiscated cell phones if students were caught using them during the school day. So it happened one day that an administrator confiscated a cell phone that a student was using. The administrator, in keeping with board policy, planned to return the cell phone after school, but shortly after taking the phone, he received a telephone call from a board member asking him to return the cell phone to the student. The administrator refused to do so. He found himself in the awkward position of honoring the board member's request or risk being accused of insubordination. This administrator, however, did not take the bait. His no-nonsense personality would not allow it. Incidences like these were common. For fear of losing their jobs, many teachers and administrators would cave in under this kind of pressure. This caused disciplinary infractions to increase in the schools. Once students figured out that teachers and administrators were afraid of board members, they relinquished any and all attempts to abide by school policy. Situations like this one also caused some administrators to surrender and let the students run the schools.

Yes, even those who were charged with establishing and enforcing policies expected administrators to comply with the most ridiculous requests, and unfortunately most of them did out of fear of retaliation. Decisions like these were nightmarish for administrators and created an environment that was uncontrollable in the schools. Situations like this one changed the attitudes of most administrators. Many would not suspend students when the situation warranted it. Regardless of the situation and circumstances, some administrators would always go easy on students because they would have gotten the message from higher-ups that they could not suspend too many of them or certain ones, depending on who their parents were.

Education is one of the most important components of one's life, and when it comes to something as important, there should not be compromises. Regardless of their fears, principals should have done more to protect their students' rights to an education even if it meant challenging the superintendent and school board. Furthermore, principals were not entirely without options. There were and always have been laws that protect educators, but few ever lodged a complaint. Some were lazy and didn't care anyway, but there were those who knew better but didn't do anything either. The unfortunate result of all this was the destruction of the learning environment and the graduation, via social promotion, of hundreds of students who simply were not prepared to go out into the world and make it on their own.

Case in point: When I was transferred to an administrative position at another school, I encountered such horrible conditions as I had never seen in any school before. A science class where the teacher was a foreigner and spoke with a deep accent was completely out of control. The majority of the students were African American. This is not to generalize about African American students, but rather, it is a factual statement about what transpired in this particular teacher's classroom. If I am to portray the realities of the classroom, I have to be honest and open, and I hope my readers will see this in the spirit in which it is intended. I want to help parents to see and understand what really happens in many of today's schools so that they will be able to pick up where schools leave off, for I sincerely believe that if parents were better informed, they would do more to help their children in these situations.

Mr. J's science class was disruptive every day. He would often arrive early to school to start his day, and part of starting would be to come to me and ask if I would be willing to visit his fourth period class where he had the most problems. I did, and on my first visit I was shocked at what I saw and heard. I had seen a lot of misconduct in the many years that I had taught, but even for me, this was a new low. Mr. J's classroom represented the kinds of things that should never happen in a school.

I have always considered myself to be tough, but this was something I had never dealt with before. The classroom was a combination of disrespect, disregard, and disruption. It was sheer madness. But rather than cave in to the total disarray, vulgarity, and insanity, my old determination and strong will of the old-school mentality kicked in. I just simply wasn't having it, but there was that small voice that kept whispering that the principal was going to undue any punishment I issued. He had a reputation for doing this, and most of the students knew that they could go and plead their cases to him, and he would take their sides. But the students were so outrageous that I had to do something. To me, it was the equivalent of walking up on a situation where someone is being stabbed. You are afraid to step in, but you know you have to do something, so you step in and get stabbed too. So I stepped in and was stabbed repeatedly. But mine was worse because I was seen as an outsider who was interfering in a situation that was not my business as they put it.

The teacher was using the projector and lecturing, and the students were supposed to be taking notes, but it was everything but that. The students were literally hanging out like they were on a street corner. Some were standing in front of the board walking around yelling while others sat on top of their desks engaging in everything from bodily contact to sucking sunflowers seeds and spitting them on the floor. And the noise level exacerbated the situation. No one could hear the teacher; his efforts were in vain, but somehow he did not seem to allow the noise to deter him from talking. He continued to talk even though no one listened. It was as if he accepted this as normal. There was no attempt on his part to get control. I did not know where to start, so I yelled to the class to come to order, get in their seats, and be quiet. My tone, commanding as it was, had no impact on their conduct. In fact, it enraged the most aggressive ones, and their ranting and raving escalated to verbal threats and many obscenities. Some walked close, circled me like animals in the wild and looked up and down as if to conjure fear in me. Their threats, though, had the opposite effect. As much as I hate to admit it, I was like them. I was bold and hid an insatiable appetite for students who thought they could tell grown folks what to do. My mouth began to water, and I was subconsciously grinding my teeth. They had brought out the animal in me (Lol). They had no idea they would be my lunch. I also knew what I had always known. In most school settings, intelligent children will back down to adults when they know they are wrong. Most of them come on really strong just to see what that adult is made of. If they detect fear, they will push it to its limit. When they see strength, especially the kind that is daring and laced with a bit of what appears to be craziness, they will back down. The average student knows when and how far to go, and they also know how to avoid being eaten alive, and some of them were able to detect the ravenous wolf in me. My physical appearance was an asset as well. I was very tall and looked a little scary, I suppose. During my tenure as a teacher, I had been told things like, "She looks like she will snatch your arm right off," or "With her appearance, she can't afford to be so mean." I imagine there was a bit of truth to some of this because I had once seen a picture of one of my aunt after she had gotten old, and she looked so mean that she looked like she could spit fire.

Working in some of the schools in the district, required a kind of strength that was unwavering and courageous. It was not what one would want, but it was what one needed. No one wants to have to go to work fearing what battles they're going to have to fight. Schools are supposed to be pleasant places where teachers enjoy teaching and students enjoy learning. But many of our schools were anything but pleasant. We had to tolerate a great deal of disrespect from administrators, parents, and students. And the thing that exacerbated the situation was the fact that we had to hide our feelings. We really couldn't complain without being accused of not being a team player. To express frustration would lead to statements that suggested one was overbearing and a potential problem or threat. As aforementioned, I often hid my real feelings about certain people and situations. It profited one nothing to show them.

Now, back to Mr. J's classroom. I suppose for the average teacher, the students in Mr. J's classroom would have posed a threat, but they were no threat to me. I was either too angry or too shocked to be afraid of them. There was an anger and frustration in me that could not be whipped by them. They wanted to see fear in me, but my experiences had not made me fearful of students. My experiences had created in me the opposite effect. Instead of fear, there was in me a resolve to hold students accountable for their conduct and discipline them. After several minutes of warnings, most of them continued what they were doing, and made comments such as "This is not your class. Get out of here. This is Mr. J's class. Mr. J, you gonna let her come in here and take over your class? You're not the principal anyway." Now that I had come in, they attempted to form an alliance with Mr. J, the man they had harassed and disrespected. He didn't fall for it, however, and I would not be chased away. I stood my ground, and instead of continuing to make demands to the entire class, I began to single out individuals and gave each explicit instructions, so that if he did not comply, I could address him, in particular, by means of a discipline referral and some form of punishment.

Most of the period was spent with students acting in open defiance and refusing to comply with instructions. Many of them egged others on by putting them in the position of escalating their violent conduct or looking like cowards. So the path that most of them took was to look like a hero. Peer pressure wouldn't let some of them back down so the classroom became a standoff, teacher versus students with Mr. J. standing close to the door and poised to run if the situation escalated to that. But he was safe because I had become the enemy now. Their beef with him was over; it was all directed at me now. Some confronted me face to face, but again, I was as tough as they were, and like they refused to comply, I refused to cower to their threats and intimidation. When they saw that I was as daring and crazy as the worst of them, some came to their senses. As I left the room, I ordered the most disruptive ones to follow me to my office. Some did and some did not. In addition to teaching, I had administrative duties, so in that position I had the authority to suspend students, and I did. I wrote discipline referrals and suspended them either home or to the in-school suspension center depending on the circumstances and hand-book policies.

After school, I went to see Mr. J. to let him know what I had done and told him that the next day should be better for him. He put on a fake smile for me. He had seen years of this and knew that it couldn't be fixed over night or probably not at all.

What little hope he might have had was short-lived. As school started the next day, those who I had suspended home walked into the building as boldly as they had walked around in his classroom the day before. They also made sure that I saw them. As they passed, I saw on their faces a smirk that said you can't do anything to us. I approached them and reminded them that they were suspended home. I told them to follow me to the office. None did. I went to the office to see the principal about the situation. This was when I learned that he had rescinded the suspensions I had given the students. I tried to explain just how outrageous they had been in their conduct. His reply was that Mr. J. was just a poor disciplinarian and that he was going to have to learn how to control his classes. He added that there was no point in trying to help him because he would not stand by any of his own decisions to punish his students. He told me that Mr. J. would often punish the students and then take it back.

The principal's decision to rescind the punishment made me feel sick, and I believed it was designed to make me give up as he was always concerned about the number of disciplinary infractions we had to enter into the state's database. Too many would eventually designate a school as "Unsafe or Dangerous," and he certainly didn't want this to happen under his watch. I felt that something had to be done, so I continued to monitor Mr. J's classroom and discipline students as necessary. I knew that the principal would rescind the punishment, but I also knew that he could not stop me from writing them up and logging them into the state's database. I also knew that it was really important for the students to know that somebody in the school cared about their conduct. For me, it was more than discipline; it sent the message that somebody cared enough to do something. In addition to this, I wanted to create in them the uncomfortable feeling of knowing that they were stacking up referrals against themselves. To do nothing, in my opinion, was a terrible injustice to them and would have long-lasting consequences. Society demands discipline, and deviants suffer. Most of them end up in jail or dead. Another very dangerous aspect of this was the fact that the principal was hiding a really bad problem. Lack of discipline had created a toxic environment in the school. The school had become a dangerous place to be because of his attempt to distort the truth by failing to report the data as was required by the state. His secrecy coupled with his failure to discipline students caused many of them to suffer. There would be wild and chaotic fights. One boy was thrown into a trophy case, and luckily he was not cut by the shattering glass. Another student's teeth were knocked out. I shall never forget the time when I suspended a student, and he decided he would come looking for me. This was a really big boy. I had caught a glimpse of him coming my way, so I used my radio to alert the principal. He wouldn't answer. I knew he had his radio because I had heard him talking minutes earlier. I needed back up, but I was being treated like the cop that others don't notice when he or she is in trouble. When I saw him later that day, I told him what had transpired, and he responded by telling me that, "Sometimes, we have to lock ourselves in." I knew the situation very well. He didn't like the fact that I was entering the disciplinary referrals into the state's database, and he didn't like the fact that I frowned on his lack of concern for the school.

I was often dismayed by the principal and his inability to recognize the importance of discipline in the school. Disciplining a child is a way of acknowledging him. It's what all parents learn when raising children. When you ignore the baby, it cries louder and louder until it gets your attention. Most of the students were seeking attention and didn't know how to get it in a positive way. So under the circumstances, I did the best I could and that was to give it to them even if it had to come in the form of punishment, for I have always believed that some attention is better than none at all, but it simply shows that you care. It is known as tough love.

I always tried to put myself in their shoes. I would think how I would feel if no one ever seemed to care about me no matter how I acted out, no matter my conduct, my rants, my outbursts. Incidences like these were common in many schools in the district. No matter how awful, some acts would be ignored. Whenever I found myself in situations like these, I always thought about "My Child" and wondered whether he had attended schools like this one where administrators ignored serious discipline problems which ultimately led to students thinking that no one cared about them no matter their conduct. Perhaps, he had, and his incarceration was just an extension of these schools. Had he been the victim of poor schools that fail to discipline students and put them on the fast track to prison? Parents can't do it all. They need the help of the schools. It still takes a village to raise a child.

Parents should know that it is so very important for them to demand the best for their children. Demand the best school leaders for them. Seek out their credentials and their attitudes in general. Visit schools often just to get a feel for the climate. Ask for conduct and disciplinary data to find out what is going on in the school. The public cannot be denied these kinds of things. Most data can be found on the state's department of education website. Most importantly, parents should follow the progress of the school from one year to the next. Ask questions such as whether there seems to be a decline in academic achievement, an increase in the number of disciplinary referrals, and a decrease in enrollment. These are red flags and should be taken seriously. I watched a school that was once vibrant and bustling with highly motivated teachers and enthusiastic students regress into one racked with discipline problems and a principal who was so self-centered that he/she put his/her personal feelings and pride above all else. He/she was either too arrogant to admit his/her shortcomings or he/she simply did not care. Either way, this principal set many students up for failure. To sum it all up, he/she never picked up on the cues that would have shown what was happening to the students and subsequently the school as a whole. Like many other administrators in the system, this principal continued to draw his/her six figure salary while all around him/her crumbled. And he/she was allowed to do so. He/she belonged to the right clique and nothing else mattered. No one held him/her accountable. It was rumored that he/she had the unwavering support of a higher up and that they enjoyed a close relationship. If this was actually the case, think of all the children whose pain was the result of their pleasure.

` I guess I should not have been surprised by the fact that parents didn't notice the extent to which a school was failing. Seldom did they visit the school. Many didn't attend PTA or come on open-house nights where they could sit and conference with teachers about their children. I remember a PTA meeting where only one parent showed up. The usual arrangement for PTA meetings was to have the parents sit on one side of the cafeteria and teachers on the other side. By the time the principal walked into the room to call the meeting to order, only one person was on the parent side. It was so embarrassing that one of our teachers who had a child attending our school, got up and joined the one parent sitting on the parent side of the cafeteria. And then my mind fell on "My Child." Were his parents like these who did not take the time to come to the school just to see what was going on? Had his parents ever visited any of his schools, or did they leave it all up to the school to raise him? If they did, they made a terrible mistake. Could this be one of the reasons "My Child" landed where he is today?

Some parents seemed not to prioritize or perhaps they didn't know how to prioritize. One would think that such a thing would be natural, but I guess it isn't.

Parents would come to the schools for trivial things such as a cell phone issue. You could always expect to see parents if their child's cell phone was taken, but seldom would they come to inquire about their children's academic performance. It was only after the children got their failing report cards when parents would come out in a rage demanding to know why teachers had failed their children. Parents and their children rarely accepted responsibility for the child's own failure. It was always the teacher's fault.

Parents don't realize the extent to which they contribute to failing schools. Parents can make or break a school. When parents come out and make outrageous and unwarranted demands of teachers and principals, they are contributing to the gradual decline of that school. I heard many times the statement, "Just let them have it. Life is going to get them anyway." Many teachers and administrators just could not deal with the outlandish conduct of parents, and thus began a subtle indifference or an attitude of complacency. Eventually, this attitude manifested in teachers giving students passing grades instead of the F's they made, failing to discipline students, telling parents what they wanted to hear, and an overall attitude of surrender. Most could not fight these battles. Thus, the saying, "Pick your battles," became well-received advice. Teachers learned to pick their battles. While many parents and their children thought they were getting over, they were actually losing. The real world was waiting for them, and unfortunately, it doesn't make alliances for those who devalue their own lives.

There were too many missed opportunities. A case in point: For years as I helped administer the state's mandated standardized tests, I watched the same students march into the testing center month after month, year after year trying to pass these tests to get their high-school diplomas. It was a sad situation. The worst of it for me was knowing that a great number of them were the victims of a poor school system that had not prepared them adequately and that they had victimized themselves as well. The sad irony of the situation was the fact that while many of them had no control over the general operations of the schools, many of them (via their conduct) had created a climate that could not prepare them to pass a standardized test to graduate.

Test results more than any other aspect of a school reveal the realities of poor schooling: teachers giving up and surrendering to parents' outrageous demands by giving unearned passing grades and administrators looking the other way instead of punishing misconduct. While students and their parents could be blamed for many of the things that went wrong in the schools, there were many things over which they had no control.

Many students attended schools that were led by incompetent administrators. Discipline problems and disruptive behavior made it impossible for teachers to teach adequately, not to mention that some students were dealing with insurmountable personal and family problems.

As I watched former students file in to take their graduation tests, I could see the embarrassment on their faces; embarrassed that they had to return time after time to retake these tests. I fought back tears, but I could feel them flowing inside me. I cried for them because I knew that it was not all their fault. But I suffered most from knowing that they didn't know it. They had been violated but were unaware. They just accepted the situation and continued to test year after year. They never complained. That youthful energy and naivety that they had when in school had been replaced with looks of seriousness and desperation. They also looked frightened and perhaps they were for they had gone out into the world and learned first- hand that they could do very little without a high-school diploma. So by now, desperation had set in. I would recognize some who had been pistols in school. The type that couldn't be controlled and would turn the class inside and out. Now, they looked like little hardened men and women who were reaching for a lifeline. I cried especially for them as it came to me slowly that these students had come to us years before too immature to recognize the importance of an education, and we had failed them. Their lives had been stolen, and they had learned too late.

I should explain what I mean when I say we had failed them. I mean that we didn't fight hard enough for them. We didn't fight the network of operations in the district that hired incompetent administrators. We didn't call out the school board for poor decision-making and poor hiring practices. We didn't call out other offices in the county that failed to address the problem of truancy. We didn't call out those superintendents who made poor decisions that impacted the district's schools.

Now, back to the testing situation. Some of the students would arrive very early and while waiting for testing to begin, would put their heads on their desks as if to hide themselves from former teachers who had taught them four or five years earlier. None stayed to chat after the tests were over. I wanted to encourage them, but the state had strict testing protocol that would not allow conversation beyond testing instructions. Furthermore, most of us administering tests had become so test weary that we barely even spoke to the students. Everything was "You can't say this, and you can't say that." So the most we could do was give them a smile and nod of encouragement.

For every good program in the school, there were many others that would undermine or sabotage any attempts to make things better for the students. I will begin with the most disastrous of them all. Whenever the district offered summer remediation programs to help struggling students, the teachers chosen to work these programs were those who did not have high failure rates. This was a system criterion. However, realistically speaking, these were the teachers who passed large numbers of failing students because they wanted to work the summer programs just for the money. Teachers who failed students during the regular school term were not chosen to teach summer school. Therefore, those who wanted to be selected to teach summer school passed almost all their students regardless of the fact that many had not done the coursework. Their actions were such a detriment to these students because these children were the ones who needed summer remediation the most, but the teachers, in just passing them, were disqualifying them for summer remediation and giving them a false sense of their capabilities and so none attended summer remediation. The few that attended were from other teachers' classes, those teachers who had failed them (given them the grades they had earned) and believed that remediation would help. The system's summer remediation programs would have probably helped the students but the programs were undermined by flawed policies and negligent teachers chosen on the basis of their low failure rates.

Some that were chosen to teach summer school were known not to teach the entire school year. It was a common sight to see them standing around socializing with others while their students were left unsupervised in their classrooms. In spite of this, they were the ones chosen to teach summer school. They had already cheated many students out of their opportunities for remediation, and now they were in a position to cripple even more during the summer months, and sadly they would be paid to do it while strong teachers who desired to work and desperately wanted to help the students were treated like failures themselves.

Summers ended for most of these children not being any better off than they were before attending remediation. For many of the teachers who taught summer school, the fruits of their false labor manifested in designer clothes or new shiny cars for themselves or their teen children or trips to the islands, a stark contrast to the living conditions of the students they'd neglected during regular school and then again in summer school.

The teachers who had high failure rates during the regular school year were actually the best teachers. They took their jobs seriously. Most of them had high failure rates because they were actually teaching and assessing students' performance. They knew their students and where they stood academically. They were the ones who refused to simply pass students for the sake of benefits, favors, and promotions. They refused to compromise their beliefs and they would not lower their standards. Unfortunately, the district did not value them, but instead, labeled them troublemakers and accused them of not being empathetic toward the students. These teachers knew the importance of grading accurately. They knew that parents should know how their children were actually doing so that they could get them the extra help they needed.

Remediation was not the only reason for summer school. Some students attended to make up for classes they had failed during the regular school year. This was a waste of time and counter-productive as well because passing summer courses was a given as long as students paid their tuition. In other words, passing grades were sold at the rate of approximately $180.00-$200.00 per course. If tuition was paid and the students did not have too many absences, passing was a guarantee. The system dared not take a chance and hire those teachers who were known to grade on the basis of student performance, so they hired the ones that they knew would pass them regardless. This was another nail in the coffin for students who were in dire need of learning. At every turn, there was another factor that sabotaged their chances of a real education. Parents knew well what the situation was in summer school, but not surprisingly, they went along with it. They expected to get the best grade their money could buy. What many did not know was that their children sat in class all-day and every day during the regular school year and made no attempt to do the work. Their money was wasted on summer school. Had they known just how little effort some put into passing, perhaps, they would not have paid for summer classes. I used to wonder what kinds of sacrifices these parents had to make to send their children to summer school. Most of these parents were poor and could not afford the cost of tuition, but they came up with the money somehow. The one thing they did not have to worry about was whether their children would pass. They all did because summer school was about money and not about learning.

Parents should take from this the importance of monitoring their children's test scores, grades, and teachers' lesson plans to determine whether teachers are covering required standards or just to get a feel for what goes on in the classroom. For example, any child with a passing grade in a course should be able to pass a state standardized test for that course because students are tested on the same standards that the state requires teachers to cover. In essence, if students are taught the standards and given periodic tests on them, they should be able to pass standardized tests based on these standards; otherwise, what would be the causes of their inability to pass unless there are undiagnosed academic deficiencies or special needs. Parents should recognize the disconnect or gap, and that is the fact that there should not be a huge difference between a student's classroom performance (his or her grades) and standardized test performance, and when these discrepancies manifest, they should ask teachers and administrators to explain them.

In case you don't make the connection, I will offer an incident that I witnessed myself. I once heard a teacher breathe a huge sigh of relief. When I looked around to see who had accomplished such a feat as to warrant such a sigh of victory, I saw a teacher who was a known slacker and was engaged in the very activity for which she had earned the nickname "hall-walker." She was walking down the hall in a state of jubilee. Report –card season was upon us, and most teachers were locked behind closed doors scrambling and focusing on getting papers graded, averaging grades, and getting them into their computers before the deadline. This teacher, though, walked the hall casually as if she had not a care in the world. As she came closer, she told me how glad she was that she had finally gotten all of her grades in the computer. Being the procrastinator she was, I was happy for her until she told me that she had not calculated any averages. I had to think about this. How could she have gotten the grades in without calculating the students' averages? In other words, what had she put into the computer? I quickly realized that she had given students grades they had not earned; she had passed all of her students. To confirm what I was thinking, I pretended not to be shocked and asked her casually how she had done it because I knew that the most hard-working and dedicated teachers had not even gotten theirs in. While she did not answer directly, her response confirmed exactly what I was thinking. Her response was that if anyone complained, she would give him or her a higher grade, but that she did not expect anyone to complain because, in her own words, "No one ever complains about a passing grade, especially those who know they have not done the work." Unfortunately, this teacher's conduct was not an isolated incident. There were others who did the same thing; the only difference was that they kept it to themselves. The irony, though, was that everybody knew because even the students would brag about not having to do the work in certain teachers' classes to pass. In addition to this, some of those same students would be the ones known for slacking off and cutting class. Some of them would have an A in one class and all F's in another. The most tragic thing about all of this was that many of these teachers taught courses where there was a required graduation test like the hall-walking teacher who taught a course that had a required graduation test, and this test was one of the most failed in our school even though most of the students had passing grades in the course itself.

    The teachers who gave unearned passing grades always made it very difficult for those who did not. After students would get their report cards and discover an F among the unearned A's B's, and C's, they would charge into the teachers' classrooms demanding to know how they had received the failing grade. Large numbers of students would pace back and forth making verbal threats at the teachers while they would be scrambling to pull folders of graded papers and absentee reports. After teachers would show them their graded papers and inform them of their total number of absences, they would settle down somewhat. Most of them knew their circumstances before inquiring. They would have already received their graded papers, and knew they had been absent and not doing classwork or homework, but they entered the classrooms attacking the teachers and thinking they could intimidate the teachers into changing the failing grade to a passing grade. They also hoped teachers did not have the evidence to support the failing grades. I always kept a folder for each student, and after returning graded papers to students, I would collect them and file them because I knew what would happen at the end of each grading period.

Many of them had become accustomed to being passed along. They never asked for graded papers in those classes where they did not have to do the work to pass. They had entered into some kind of psychological alliance with these teachers with the understanding that, "as long as she passes me, I won't bother her. I want question anything; I'll leave her alone." They did not seem to care that they were not learning anything. They never realized that the real enemies were the teachers who just passed them on. They did not know that these teachers were crippling them for life. They did not know to what extent the conduct of these teachers was a detriment to their future, particularly in our society that bases a person's worth on his or her educational attainment. And, what about "My Child?" Had most of his teachers been the kind that just passed him on? Had he been the victim of lazy teachers and social promotion?

The teachers, of course, knew they were doing these students a terrible disservice, but some did not care. There were many students with passing grades in their coursework who could not pass the graduation tests, so they were no better off. They were not going anywhere. It would have been better if the teachers had given them the grades they had actually earned. At least they would not have been carrying the false notion that they could perform, only to learn later (when it really counted) that they could not perform well enough to graduate. Failing just one test meant that a student could not graduate high school regardless of grade point average.

Passing failing students was not the only obstacle to student achievement. At every turn, there was another attempt to beat the system. In the case of athletes, many of these students were the most exploited of all students. These were the football, basketball players, and track stars who dreamed of playing professional sports. Many of them were really good players, and this, more than any other, was an excellent opportunity for the coaches to drive home the importance of academics, to get these students to really study and perform as well in the classroom as they did on the field, court, and track and some coaches did just that like Coach Truitt and his staff, but there were some who tried to beat the system especially when it came to the state's policy of "No-pass-no-play."

The "No-pass-no-play" policy stated that student athletes must pass five of his or her six classes to be eligible to participate in any competitive sport. But many athletes failed and became ineligible, so someone created a seventh class. This gave the athletes a cushion. They could fail two classes and would still be eligible. As long as they had passed five, they could play. No one knew who created the seventh course, but many athletes took advantage of it. The sad fact of this is that some coaches did not use the "No-pass-no-play" policy to motivate students to work hard and achieve academically. Instead, they found a way to get around it. And the worst of it was that the seventh course was generally a nothing course like conditioning, weight training, or study hall. I am not appointing the finger at any coach in particular. I really can't remember who the athletic director was during this time. As I have already mentioned, I worked at this school for over two decades.

My advice to parents is that you should hold coaches accountable for your children's academic success, and coaches should want for their athletes what they want for their own children. To clarify, I will share a personal story that drives home the point I am trying to make. I once taught a coach's son who was an "A" student. Many years earlier, this same coach had tried to convince a parent to take her son out of my class because he was failing. The young man was playing ball for the coach. The parent did not take him out. His grades eventually improved and the parent was pleased that she had not taking him out of my class. Many years later, I saw this parent, and she recalled the incident with her son. She expressed how glad she was that she had not taken him out of my class. As we continued to talk, I told her that I had taught the coach's son years after her son had graduated. I shall never forget the look on her face. She was obviously dismayed. Her words to me were that if she ever saw him again, she was going to let him know what she had learned. This parent experienced the cruel awakening that coaches do not always have the best intentions for their players. I guess she realized, in that instant, that he was only concerned about her son being eligible to play ball and that he wanted his son in my class because he knew that I set the bar high and would require students to perform to pass. This book is also written for the parent and her son who has since passed away. The only thing I can offer her is the truth and that is that parents should not take it for granted that coaches care about their children. Many of them just simply want to win games and get the rewards that come as a result. I thought about "My Child" and wondered had he too been the victim of a careless coach. All of this reminds me of these rappers who captivate children with their lyrics and sell them the notion that a hard life is the best life all the while doing everything in their power to make sure their children don't follow their footsteps. They want theirs to go to college and live by the rules of society because they know that anything else brings too much pain and suffering; yet they infiltrate the minds of the poor and misguided and profit from them at the same time.

So what should parents take from this? Parents should know that nobody else is going to do for their children what they can and should do. They must be personally invested in their children's education. In addition to this, parents should not settle for their children just passing, but rather, conference with teachers and require them to show graded papers that support passing grades. Sure, it's convenient for children to pass, and every parent wants to believe that his or her child is ready to move on to the next level whether it's a higher grade, college or the job market, but the truth is, without a solid education, children are destined to fail.

Students' false sense of their capabilities made them apply for college, and those who were able to pass the graduation tests actually got in because they had good grades (many of them were gifts), but they could not stay because they could not do the coursework. Many could not function at the high-school level, so it came as no surprise to others that they could not function at the college level. They had bought in to the hype that they were ready for college. They did not know that unearned passing grades were equally dangerous and destructive as their denial of their capabilities. Many believed that the unearned A's and B's were earned. Perhaps for them, it was much easier to pretend than face the truth. Most of them lived lives of pretense and theirs was a world of pretend. The real world requires real effort, intense studying, and sacrifice; qualities most of them lacked. I must add that these statements don't apply to every student. There were many students who were hard-working and dedicated to their studies. They were goal-oriented and destined for success. Some went on to become doctors, lawyers, teachers, and cooperate executives, but too many of them missed opportunities and failed to take their futures seriously.

Too many of these students ended up back home and clueless in terms of what happened. They found themselves back at the same fast food restaurants where they worked when in high school. These situations were oftentimes compounded by the fact that many now had families of their own to support. It was not uncommon to drive through a fast-food line and see some students who had left school many years earlier. Some would be polite and speak, and others would hang their heads in shame as if they did not want to be recognized.

There is an essence to learning that everyone should experience, and sadly some students were cheated out of this as well. That thing is the special feeling, the one that hooks a person and makes him fall in love with the challenge of learning new and difficult things. It is the ecstasy and reward that come after one has studied long and hard those difficult concepts such as those taught in courses like statistics, calculus, and chemistry, and then the realization that he has it; that he understands it. This, more than any other lesson, teaches the value of hard work and motivates the spirit to stay the course. Students did not get to experience this mystical and magical moment because they did not have to study to pass in some of their classes. In essence, they did not get to feel that moment of pure joy at having won a hard-fought battle. It is the thing that teaches the student to have confidence in himself and validates that he is capable of accomplishing difficult tasks. No one should be robbed of that experience.

The important advice for parents is to show just as much concern for A's, B's, and C's as for D's and F's, as this might save your child in the long run. The very thing that might seem a blessing today, could be a curse tomorrow. Parents should not just settle for passing. They should demand to know how and why their child passed.

Again, parents are reminded of the dangers of teachers who just pass students along. Many of them have no expectations and will just pass students to avoid confrontations with parents and administrators who pressure them to pass students. Unfortunately, some teachers pass them along so they do not have to teach them. Students do not study for these teachers. They do not attend after-school tutorials or seek any extra help because they know they are going to pass regardless. This is so very tragic in that they are getting a false sense of their capabilities and at the same time, they are cheating themselves out of the help they need to really overcome their academic deficiencies.

Parents should realize what all teachers know and that is when students do not study at the lowest level (classwork) they are doing a great deal more than neglecting schoolwork. Basically, they are neglecting their entire future. Classwork is the very lowest level of life preparation. The school years are the easiest and the simplest of life tasks. All that comes later is the difficult part of life. There is a pattern in life, a cycle so to speak, and this cycle can be vicious.

To summarize, there is the simplest and easiest work, then there are state requirements designed to make students prove they are worthy of a high-school diploma, i.e. the states' required graduation tests. A student either passes or he does not. Simple as it seems, it is actually one of the most impacting aspects of one's life, and it has far-reaching consequences. If the student does not get his high-school diploma, he does not get any kind of a decent job if he gets one at all. He probably cannot even get into the military. In spite of this, this person matures into adulthood. As nature would have it, he now has all the wants and needs that naturally accompany adulthood: relationships, then children, and a need for resources for family, but there are none. There is no money and no way of getting any, and then desperation sets in and then the only opportunity available to him as he sees it is to prey on others, which leads to him or her committing crimes. This is when this once cute little dapper who laughed and slept, played and clowned in class and drew laughter and high fives from his classmates turns to drugs and snorting and gang- banging and lying and snatching and stealing and robbing and burglarizing and being arrested and bonded and making court appearances and being sentenced and convicted and spending years in prison and being paroled and repeating the cycle for years and becoming institutionalized forever, seeing prison as normal and accepting it as home because it is the only factor that is consistent in his life. Now, this once cute little person eats and sleeps at someone else's expense. Then, there are those he left behind. They have nothing, so the cycle begins again. Perhaps, this happened to "My Child." Had he also been put on the fast track to prison?"

My advice to parents is to take a long hard look at your babies and ask yourselves, "Could this really happen to my child?" My answer is yes; it could be your child in the next ten to fifteen years. It usually does not take that long. It all depends on where your child is now and what he or she is doing at this moment. Do you know whether your child is in a good school where the principal demonstrates good leadership and where the teachers are teaching and there are high standards and even higher expectations? Can you say definitively that your child is in that kind of environment? If you cannot, your child is in trouble. Any child can become a victim of a poor school. It does not matter how well he or she is raised or how much he or she is loved. Life has no mercy on people who don't prepare for their future and settle for mediocrity..

People generally think of convicts as people who were raised in poor neighborhoods, those who were exposed to violence and crime as children, young boys and girls raised in homes without fathers and mothers who loved them. While some of this might be true, this is not always the case. Some convicts come from good homes. Some have siblings who are very successful people. The difference is what they choose to do with their lives. If they reject educational opportunities in their simplest and easiest forms, then they choose this vicious cycle. While their parents and teachers play a huge role in all of this, they are the ones who ultimately determine their fate. The fact remains, however, that teachers and administrators, as people who are mandated and expected to do their jobs in preparing students for the real word should act as if these students are their own children, but in many instances, they don't.

Another sad set of circumstances that corrupted the schools was the total disregard or lack of respect for those people who were put in place to lead the charge of educating students. These people were the principals, their assistants, curriculum supervisors, instructional coaches, lead teachers, and departmental chairpersons. Because many teachers regarded them as nothing more than incompetent people who were promoted to high level positions via the buddy system, they did not respect them or acknowledge them, and I cannot say that the teachers were totally wrong because the system had compromised its reputation with its hiring practices. Even though some of these leaders were smart and competent people, many teachers felt that they were elevated to positions for which they were unqualified to hold. In some instances, even the principals themselves would not support and respect the positions of other school leaders. For example, some principals felt threatened by those who were really smart and instead of accepting them and allowing them to take the challenge, they used their authority to hinder and impede their progress; some going as far as to impress upon the teachers that they did not have to comply with directives given by certain other leaders. This attitude in principals brought schools to a standstill. There would be no gains because the school principal him/herself would have sabotaged or undermined those practices that would have contributed to academic gains.

Many schools were run by incompetent and vicious administrators who had an axe to grind. Administrators would start but would not follow through on their plans for improvement, and many teachers felt that it was a total waste of their time to start something that they knew would be forgotten in the next couple of months. There were countless initiatives that were doomed and rendered dead from the onset. They also knew that administrators would back down and not follow through with the best of practices depending on the people connected with the initiative even though some were specifically designed for the safety of the overall school.

A case in point: The last day of school offered many challenges. This would be the day that students would use to settle old scores. There would be talk of gang fights and other altercations. To say that the last day was volatile is an understatement. Administrators had to be extra careful and work diligently to have an uneventful closing, and so they worked hard at it. They would create a schedule that released students at staggered intervals at the end of the day. For release, students would be divided into categories. Walkers would be called together and sent on their way, and other categories such as bus riders and then drivers would follow in ten –to-fifteen minute intervals. The purpose was to create some distance between the groups so that there would not be large numbers of students on campus at the same time. All of the teachers would be responsible for ushering the students out of the building as quickly as possible, and administrators and coaches would be waiting outside the school to get them off campus until all of the students were gone. Generally, the process worked smoothly but with one exception.

After all the intense effort to get the students out of the building, there would be one student who would walk through the hall boldly in front of all the teachers who would be out in the hallway celebrating the success of the smooth release. His appearance suggested that we had not been so successful after all. It was an act of defiance that no one challenged because his mother worked at the school. Most teachers would be upset because they knew what he was doing. He was validating that he was beyond reproach because he knew no one would dare challenge the behavior of a student whose parent worked in the school. His actions were a display of students' relentless effort to ignore and defy school policies. He felt that because his mother worked there, he really did not have to comply and so he did not. Even though his mother worked in the school, he could have stayed in her office until the two of them left together, but instead, he chose to parade in front of the teachers in some kind of parade of victorious celebration of being able to defy authority and get away with it.

Acts like these were common in the school. Someone was always challenging authority or seeking some kind of special treatment. Perhaps, some of them were seeking validation of themselves and wanted to feel special. These things destroyed the fabric of the school because leaders ignored these things when colleagues' children were the culprits. Perhaps, no one wanted to embarrass a colleague, but ignoring the situation only made it worse because other students adopted the attitude that if he could do whatever he wanted to do in the school, they could as well.

The students were not the only deviants. Teachers had their moments as well. For example, school leaders would meet for hours after school discussing problems and laying out plans to solve them, only to have them later ridiculed and ignored by teachers. Teachers ignored them because they knew they would not be reprimanded, and they were right. All of these well laid-out plans came without any accountability mechanism. Administrators would neither monitor their expectations nor reprimand those who would not comply. As a result, the problems in the schools escalated.

A case in point: In a school-improvement meeting, the principal expressed anger at the number of students lingering in the hallways after the tardy bell. These students, according to the principal, were making no real attempt to get to class on time, so the committee came up with a plan. The principal and his staff decided that teachers should close their doors after the last bell and instead of allowing late students to enter the classroom, they would send them to the "tardy room" so that they could get unexcused tardy slips. The idea was that after students accumulated a certain number of these unexcused tardies, they would be suspended home. The principal began this new system with an announcement over the intercom informing both teachers and students of the new tardy policy. The first day of implementation was met with enthusiasm by some teachers and indifference by others. For every one teacher who put forth an honest effort to support the new tardy policy, there would be three others who openly defied it by letting late students walk right into the classroom after the tardy bell. Teachers standing right next to each other would be at odds with the students. While one would try to send a late student to the tardy room to get a tardy pass, the other would just let his or her late student walk in while the other student stood there in strong protest making accusations about the unfairness of the teacher who was trying to enforce the policy. Students could be heard shouting, "See, she let hers in; Why are you trying to stop me. Get out of my way," and some who were bold enough would slip right by their teacher as she gazed at the other teacher who was allowing her students to walk in freely.

The new tardy policy was doomed from the start. For some teachers, the battle with the students was too fierce. There were also those who would not be on board because they had seen too many failed attempts to change things and had given up on the idea of real change. There were also those who knew that because there would not be a hundred percent participation, the plan would not work anyway. The paraprofessional, for example, whose job it was to manage the tardy room, did anything but manage it. He allowed the few who were sent to the tardy room to walk out at will. This meant that they would not get tardy slips, so there would be no record of their tardies, which meant that they would go unpunished. Some of these students would go back to their classes and lie to their teachers telling them things like "They're not writing tardy passes;" "They told us to go on to class." Most teachers would let them in because they would be too busy to argue with them or call the office for verification. They would let them in the classrooms even though there would be no announcement stating that they should do so.

The new tardy policy actually increased the number of tardies. It failed in many ways, but the worst was in the message it sent to students. It was reaffirmation that they could beat the system, not only with the tardy policy, but with other policies as well. It reaffirmed their thinking that teachers did not follow policy either. It compromised the principal's authority and made him appear weak and ineffective. The principal's mistake was that he thought the teachers would naturally comply since the policy would make things better for them. He could not have been more mistaken.

The fact is that not all teachers have a stake in school improvement. Some have no interest in the very schools in which they are a part. Sadly, many are there just to get a paycheck. Now, there is nothing wrong with being paid, but there is something definitely wrong with being paid for doing nothing.

Noncompliance was definitely a toxic factor in our school; however, I feel there is also a kind of truth, as uncomfortable as it is to admit (because it lets some teachers off the hook) that cannot be ignored, and that is the teachers' truth. Many were tired and weary. Some things made it impossible for them to do their jobs. Many of them were aggravated by what they considered to be the hiring of unqualified administrators such as buddies, sorority sisters, fraternity brothers, and incompetent family members. Talent and merit had nothing to do with hiring and promotions, and the teachers knew it. Perhaps, their frustration would not have been so great if there were none better, but there were many qualified people who could have done much better, and the teachers knew it.

There was another school in the system that was run by a principal who was weak and had a bad reputation among parents and students. This principal could not discipline the students because he had put himself in a compromising position and parents knew too much about him. This principal, however, was surrounded by very strong men and women who had the reputation, respect, and tenacity to get the job done, but his insecurities and thirst for power would not allow him to solicit their support. Instead, he ignored them and caused the school to sink to a level of non-redemption. The students even seemed to take pride in the fact that their school was reputed as the worst in the system, and they even coined a nickname for themselves. I won't give it here to protect the guilty. None were innocent.

There was another school that was run by an elementary school principal who was sent to a high school because of an ethics issue. This principal knew absolutely nothing about high school. She had spent the majority of her tenure as an elementary school principal, but she belonged to the "clique" so instead of giving her the axe, the "powers-that-be" promoted her. She made a much higher salary as a high-school principal. Thus, another instance of someone being paid to do nothing. The thing that was worse than doing nothing was the fact that she caused the school to regress. Before she became principal, our school would provide tutorials for students who would be taking the high-school graduation tests. In one particular subject area (I won't name it here), the students would meet as a group with their teachers, and tutorials would be provided, but because she had been named in an ethics violation, she ended the tutorial. She did so even though there was no real reason to discontinue it. We even got the approval of our school improvement specialist who was assigned to our school. As we expected, when we received our scores, they had decreased tremendously from previous years. In previous years, scores in this department were high. I really blamed the school board far more than I blamed her. After all, they had approved the hiring of this person to a position for which she was not qualified.

To sum it up, this principal's tenure at the high school was marked by a decrease in students' test scores, low morale among faculty, demotions, firings of good teachers, playing favorites, and a great number of other bad decisions and acts. The worst thing about her leadership or lack thereof was the way she played favorites with her buddies. Good teachers were ruined under her leadership. None of them did any more than they had to do. On a regular basis, they would be caught standing in the hallway having casual conversations while their students sat in the classrooms and did nothing. And I should not use the word "caught" because no one ever caught them. No one tried to catch them because they were the principal's buddies. They could do no wrong in her eyes. They knew she wouldn't say or do anything to redirect them. Borrowing from the students, I guess I should say, "She had their backs."

One of the worst acts of favoritism I recall was an incident that involved selecting "Teacher of the Year." The "Teacher- of- the –Year" selection process was designed so that teachers could select one of their own to recognize for a job well done, even though in some cases, it was common knowledge that the principal would make the final decision. This, of course, was a violation but no one dared complain for fear of retaliation.

The selection process began with teachers making nominations on secret ballots. From the ballots, a list was compiled by the principal and a few in her cohort. By the time this list would make it around to the teachers, they would be suspicious because in talking with others, they would learn that many of their nominations would not be on the principal's list. Teachers were naturally suspicious because their nominations were left off the list. Teachers were forced to vote for the names on the principal's list which many were reluctant to do because some of these people were her buddies who were not required to do anything. They were not the teachers who were really going above and beyond to comply with state mandates. I knew this because I worked directly with the teachers and observed them often.

The principal's list contained the names of some of her friends who complained constantly and stood around in the hallway and did nothing. They made few attempts to comply with state mandates. Even though compliance was a challenge, there were those teachers who completed the tasks. Their classrooms reflected the state standards and were evidence of their commitment to the students and the overall success of the school. Their names, however, were not the ones on the principal's list. This was the greatest injustice of all and such a slap in the face to those teachers who were doing their jobs. It was such an unfortunate thing that the principal whose job it was to lead the charge of implementation was the person who undermined it. I was so disgusted with this that I decided to speak to the principal about it. As I was not one of her favorite people, I decided it would be better if I emailed her instead. My email basically reminded her how hard it had been to accomplish the task of getting teachers to comply with state guidelines regarding the standards-based classroom. I told her that to select a teacher who had not accomplished these tasks would be a total disregard for state policies and would send the message that compliance was not important in our school.

I was concerned about the message. Basically, we were saying that state mandates were not important in the school if a teacher could ignore them and be rewarded for it. I thought this was totally irresponsible on the part of the principal. My plea went unheard, and it enraged her. She responded to my email by saying that the job of selecting "Teacher of the Year" was for the teachers and that she would not interfere with it. She was right in this except the teachers were not given the opportunity to do this. It was her list. I did not feel that the teachers really cared whether one of her buddies would be designated "Teacher-of-the-Year" as long as that person was someone who had done the work and deserved the designation. This was seen by teachers as just another instance of irresponsible conduct committed by a principal. For example, in a previous year, there had been an incident in which a non-certified substitute teacher had been selected as "Teacher-of-the-Year." It was like designating a law clerk "Attorney-of-the-Year."

The principal's buddies paraded around as if they were invincible, and under her leadership they were. The most unfortunate and tragic thing about these acts was that the students would be the ones who would suffer the most. They would be the ones who would not be able to compete; not even with their own relatives who were attending better schools in the same district. They would be poor and desperate and depending on their parents for the rest of their lives. Many of them would end up on drugs and incarcerated like "My Child." They would move on to nowhere while those charged with educating them continued their lavished lifestyles with their six figure salaries that made it possible for them to have designer clothes, luxury cars and nice suburban homes. When I think of their lives in relation to the students whose lives they stole, I am often reminded of Shakespeare's statement in "The Tragedy of Julius Caesar" where he contends that the upper-class climbs the ladder of success on the backs of the underclass and once they ascend to their destination, they look back down on the poor whose backs they used and they "scorn the base degrees upon which they did ascend." Yes, on the backs of these poor children, many educators climbed the ladder to success and left the little ones to fend for themselves. Thus, the saying, "I got mine; you got to get yours" was an accurate portrayal of the attitudes of some educators in our district's schools.

Advice to parents: Stop the hero worship. Many parents are blinded by the "nice" syndrome. As long as the principal or teachers present themselves as "nice" then they feel these people cannot do any wrong. They don't question them, or worse, they don't hold them accountable. Some parents never seemed to care about anything other than whether the person facing them was nice. Nothing else mattered as long as the teachers and principals were nice. Being nice is pleasant, but that should not excuse a person from doing his or her job. Being nice does not educate children and neither does it discipline them. In fact, it can actually be counterproductive especially in situations where tough love would be more effective.

It was not unheard of for teachers to present this façade as a means of deflecting from the real problems in the schools. A lead teacher, for example, once stated that "All you have to do is get the parents on your side." I did not know exactly what he intended, but I interpreted it to mean that once you get the parents on your side, then you don't have to do much more. Considering the fact that he was a special education teacher where there was an even greater need for dedicated and hardworking teachers, his comment was actually scary. Unfortunately, he was not alone in his thinking. There were many teachers who tried to kill everything and everybody with kindness. And unfortunately, it was the students' lives that were stolen. They were killed by kindness. Had "My Child" also died from the disease known as "kindness?"

Some teachers were better at killing than others. They would pull all kinds of antics. None of which had anything to do with educating students. There were several who seldom engaged their students academically but were always involved in some aspect of their social lives. For example, in social settings involving the students, they were a bit too child-like themselves. It was as if they wanted to be friends with the students. Personally, I just feel like teachers and administrators should limit their relationships to professional when it comes to students. I feel it is alright to be friendly, but students should see educators as professionals who are always available and there to support them. Some of our principals, however, were willing to overlook friendly relationships with students because some probably felt that teachers' love for the students was genuine, and some of them desperately needed this kind of love and attention from their teachers.

Regarding duties and responsibilities, teachers should never neglect their duties and responsibilities when it comes to educating students. Nothing can replace a good solid education. It doesn't matter how nice a teacher is or how willing he or she is to listen to students, council them, or socialize with them. Educating them should be a teacher's main goal. Teachers should be dedicated to improving their lives by teaching them. No one can take away a good education. Once a student acquires a good education, he/ she has it for life. It becomes the stepping stone for many other important aspects of life.

Concerning the "nice" approach aforementioned, there are two sides to most stories, and it is my intention to present both sides even if it seems a bit contradictory. The other side of this story was the fact that some administrators had to resort to this approach to protect themselves against uncontrollable irate parents who would come to the schools seeking to settle conflicts on their own terms. It was not uncommon for a parent to attack an administrator. There were instances where school security had to forcibly remove parents from the schools' grounds. In very volatile situations like these, principals naturally tried to diffuse the situations by being calm and nice. Situations like these were understandable because administrators had very little choice in these matters, but under ordinary circumstances, a deliberate attempt to deceive parents by deflecting from the real issues was wrong, and many administrators did just that.

My advice to parents is that you should present yourselves as caring and concerned and less of a threat; however, you should also carry yourselves in a manner that suggests to teachers and administrators that you're concerned about your child's overall well-being. You should send the message that you're not willing to sacrifice your child for the sake of cordial relationships. The best way to do this is to ask relevant questions and request documentation and evidence that support what they tell you.

One of the worst things you can do is back administrators into a corner. When you come off as impatient, overbearing, and threatening, administrators are going to protect themselves, and they will only tell you whatever they feel you want to hear or just enough to calm you. This, of course, won't be the truth. You shouldn't force this deception by attacking principals. If you present yourselves as caring people, principals will be less inclined to distort the truth and more inclined to have an honest discussion about the things that are taking place, and will probably solicit your support in an effort to improve things.

As a mentor, I experienced many different kinds of people and situations. My schedule was fairly routine and mainly involved observing teachers and conferencing with them afterwards. I generally approached each situation with an attitude of genuine concern and willingness to assist whenever and wherever I was needed. I was never overbearing or unreasonable. Before becoming a mentor, I had been in the classroom for many years, and I knew well the challenges involved, so I positioned myself as a cheerleader for the teachers and their biggest supporter; however, I quickly learned that no amount of love, support, and professionalism is enough for people who do not like you. While there were many teachers who appreciated my effort, there were those who scorned my very existence and did not pass on any opportunity to remind me of that fact. A case in point: I once observed a teacher who was really close with a principal who had no love for me. On the day that I walked into her classroom, it was an aimless mess. The students sat and talked idly while others worked at pulling posters from the wall, storing books, and attending to other school-closing tasks. School would close in about a month, but this teacher was already closing out her year. I did not leave because they were cleaning the room. I stayed and observed her class regardless. To avoid getting in their way, I took what I considered to be a safe seat in a corner, as I was not one of her favorite people. After about ten minutes, the teacher rushed over to me as if she could not take it any longer and said, "You have to move; I need this seat." I recognized her intent; therefore, I moved quietly to another seat and continued taking notes on my clipboard. Before long, this teacher walked over and whispered to me, "You don't have to give me a copy because I'm not going to read it anyway." By this, she meant that she was not going to read my comments. I would always leave a copy of my observation form with the teachers as a matter of record and for them to read over so that they could improve deficiencies if that was the case. This teacher knew that she could get away with this because of her relationship with the principal. She could not have cared less about my suggestions and whether her cooperation and subsequent changes would benefit her students. She simply did not like me, and she certainly was not going to take my suggestions. After all, as far as she was concerned, school had closed and the principal "had her back." Unfortunately, this incident was just a chip off the old block. This teacher was known to act unprofessionally and display total disregard for school leaders. In a separate incident, she attacked and belittled an assistant principal, and bragged about it in a departmental meeting in front of her colleagues. Teachers had come to the meeting expecting the usual business, but were shocked when they heard her bragging about how she had "cussed out" Mr._____, who was an administrator. She went on to say how she had planned to use the "M" and "F" words. And the worst of it was the statement she made in the presence of others, "If he doesn't think I have clout in this town, he needs to ask somebody who my daddy is." Her declaration was a reflection of the attitudes of many others. It was common. One's connections with certain others in the community would be a pass to act up or say and do just about anything and get away with it. Promotions and many other job opportunities were determined by a person's connections with certain others in the community. Ability and talent had little to no basis for a promotion. In some instances, promotions were so obviously wrong that most people just threw their hands up in surrender to the madness. The statement, "Just let them have it," became a common declaration of the teachers' disgust with it all. Thus, morale was always at an all –time low, and many teachers just counted the years until they had enough to retire with a decent salary or, in the case of younger teachers, many sought jobs in other fields, even if it meant they would have to go back to college and start from scratch. For many of them, teaching was not worth all the politics and low salary. They were exhausted by all of the biased practices and improprieties.

One of our administrators was a total disaster, and his lack of leadership brought our school to an all-time low. He would have teachers go head-to-toe with students about their conduct in his presence and then side with the student depending on the teacher involved. In a conference, a teacher would vehemently express what a student had done in class. All the while, he would stand there listening. The student, of course, would deny the accusations. I recall an incident when I assigned after-school detention to a student who had erased my notes from the board after I stepped outside the classroom to conference with another student. When I stepped back into the classroom, I naturally inquired about the erased board. No one said anything. After that, I tore strips pf paper and gave one to each student. I asked them to write the name of the student who had erased the board. After checking the slips, I saw that one name appeared more than others. After class, in a one-on-one conference with the student, I informed him that his name had appeared more than once. After that he admitted to erasing the board and accepted his punishment which was after-school detention. I was proud of him for owning his deed and accepting responsibility for it. However, on the day of detention, he did not show up. I was forced to take him to see the principal. On the way, we met the principal in the hallway. I explained to him what had transpired. The student listened as intently as the principal and didn't deny anything. After I finished, the principal looked at the student and told him that he was not under any obligation to stay for after-school detention because I was outside the classroom when the incident happened and that I did not see him do it. I was shocked at the principal's statement, and the student seemed equally shocked, but there was no celebratory air around the student. He walked slowly back to the classroom with me as if he was apologetic and afraid. It was as if he had won a prize that he did not want but could not give back. This incident seemed to have changed the student. Prior to, he was lively and just an ordinary kid. Afterwards, he seemed more mature and concerned, and his child-like innocence was no more. The principal, however, was not innocent. He had intended to humiliate me in the presence of the student. This was the same man whose advances I had rejected on numerous occasions. He was a hugger, but I never hugged him. I had to be creative and come up with all kinds of excuses. I would tell him that I did not want to get make-up on his snow-white shirt. He would laugh and say that I would say anything to avoid hugging him. The truth was that I wanted him to respect me as a teacher and not see me as a woman there for his personal gratification. Besides, he never made such passes at the white female teachers. They were treated like professionals. Whenever they turned students in for disciplinary infractions, he would punish the students. The principal's support of the white teachers made it appear that they were better teachers than the black teachers, so many parents wanted their children to have white teachers. The principal would accommodate these parents by assigning the smartest blacks to white teachers for Advanced Placement courses and other students would be assigned to black teachers in basic courses. Parents of these children either did not know or they did not care because they never questioned the assignment of certain classes to certain teachers.

The beginning of each year ushered in a host of newly promoted school administrators. In most districts, this would have been a welcomed and positive move, but quite the opposite for our school district. Instead of teachers experiencing that rush of excitement "that this year will be better than the last because of the possibility of each new school year opening the doors to new ideas, opportunities, and increased awareness with new leaders," teachers felt a rush of anxiety as the new assistant principals were introduced. Their fears were usually justified.

In the thirty plus years that I worked in the system, I witnessed the hiring of many unqualified and incompetent administrators. Among the many, there were some whose conduct was so bad that I absolutely have to mention them. The first, our call AP 1. He was loud and obnoxious and a total embarrassment to the field of education. I think it's fair to say that he almost changed the course of teaching and administrative history. All that we had experienced and learned over the years, was changed in an instant either because he was too arrogant to listen to others, or he was of the opinion that being an administrator made him a dictator. He gave bad advice, abandoned common sense, and took pleasure in it.

A case in point: In a parent conference, he insinuated that a teacher was wrong to refer to a student as "bad." After the parent conference, he met with the teacher and told her that the term should not be used when referring to students. He admonished the teacher for telling the parent that her child was "bad." But this was exactly what the boy was, bad. In fact, he was worse than bad. He was out of control. The teacher was calling his conduct what it actually was to present a clear picture to the parent. The teacher could not bring herself to lie about it or downplay the situation because his conduct was interfering with her ability to teach and manage her classroom, so she said that he was bad. She could have said worse. She could have said that he was destructive because every time she would bring her class to a controllable point where she could teach, he would disrupt the class as if he wanted to send the message that he was in charge and not her.

Situations like these eventually destroyed the fabric of the school's climate. They created fear among teachers and ripped from them their ability to be honest and forthcoming with parents, and needless to say, these things always made matters worse for the teachers because administrators saw their concern and intolerance as being insubordinate, and they had the authority to write letters of insubordination and put them in teachers' personnel folders. These letters could have followed teachers for the rest of their careers. It did not matter that they were contrived and the result of an overly zealous administrator who was above being questioned. Most administrators had the unwavering support of the superintendent who had been given the job (not selected by the school board from a pool of applicants) and most of the people he/she chose to run the schools were those who would fall in line and question nothing, right or wrong. His/her tenure as superintendent had taken the district back decades where fearful blacks questioned nothing and followed orders even when those orders made things difficult for the teachers and students in their schools.

The most overbearing principals were the older ones who had not gone to integrated schools as students themselves. They were intimidated by whites, and their leadership styles reflected it. They never questioned anything that came from whites, but had no problem "putting blacks in their place."

Administrators like these caused schools to decline irreversibly. After five or six years of such leadership, most schools could not recover, so schools became baby-sitting services that held children all day until their parents picked them up in the afternoon. Schools were drained by this poor leadership. Students were disruptive, teachers were burned out, and many parents were appreciative of the free baby-sitting services that were paid for by the hard-earned dollars of taxpayers.

Advice to parents: Be aware of principals like the one that admonished the teacher for referring to the student as bad. This principal did not like this teacher and had never turned down an opportunity to humiliate her. Do not always fall for what seems an easy fix. Whenever you are called for a parent conference, know that the situation is serious.

Teachers do not generally call for parents unless the situation warrants it. They simply do not have the time to call unnecessary conferences. Most do not like parent conferences anyway because of their experiences with dishonest administrators who support parents in the face of teachers even when they are wrong. Be suspicious of administrators whose attitude and tone are not in line with the teacher's. Many administrators like to downplay the seriousness of situations. Oftentimes, they are more concerned about the school's image than they are about you and your child. Put more trust in what the teacher is saying. After all, he or she is trying to make the situation better by creating conditions that will allow him or her to teach. I would further suggest that you discipline your child and see to it that the school acts as an extension of the disciplinary measures you are taking at home. For example, if there are certain people you don't allow your child to associate with outside of school, then solicit the help of administrators and ask that they do not allow these relationships in school. Most will assist you to the best of their ability. Collaboration and corporation are key. Do not be shy about letting school administrators know your feelings regarding what they are doing and whether their strategies are in line with what you are trying to accomplish with your child. In addition to these things, create a positive relationship with teachers. Some teachers are good people who care about children but face many obstacles in trying to do their jobs. The good ones give it their all, but unfortunately, they belong to a profession that is undervalued and blamed for student failure. Theirs is the profession with the smallest salaries and the least amount of appreciation. In all honesty, they are parents outside the home. They help in unimaginable ways. I am sure you can recall a teacher who made a real difference in your life.

The ability to reason and use common sense are the most impacting aspects of successful leadership. While educational experience and background are important, they are not the mechanisms that force appropriate actions and reactions. School administrators who exude a great deal of common sense and ability to reason are the driving forces behind successful schools, especially in times of crisis when these qualities generally manifest themselves. The ability to make good and sound decisions are key components in the successful operations of a school. Unfortunately, too many school leaders are lacking in these areas. A great deal of school failure can be linked directly to leaders who lack the ability to reason. Many of our schools' problems could be linked directly to those administrators who were either incapable of thinking logically or were too proud to listen to others who could. Many of them sacrificed the students and teachers for their own selfish pride. Take for example instances when administrators dealt with disruptive students. All administrators, teachers, students, and parents were given a student handbook at the beginning of each school year. Students were given copies to take home, and they along with their parents would sign a form in acknowledgement of having been informed of the school's policies and procedures. The point of all this was to inform students and parents of the consequences of misconduct and failure to adhere to school policy.

Generally speaking, a student handbook is considered the key element in creating a positive school climate, but unfortunately, in our district, it did nothing of the sort. It carried no weight. It meant nothing to students because they had learned that administrators did not always use it. They knew it existed in name only. After all, when they fought and would be given in-school suspension instead of out-of-school-suspension as the policy stated, they knew that the handbook was just another tool that administrators used in any manner they chose. Oftentimes, it depended on the person involved. If the student was a popular athlete, then perhaps nothing much would happen. On the other hand, if the student was on the principal's hit list, then he would throw the book at him. He could be suspended home for a week for the same infraction that would have landed another student in in-school-suspension. These inconsistencies in discipline destroyed school climate, opened the doors of discontent, and ruined the reputations of many schools in the district. There were parents who would threaten to sue the system because of disparaging treatment. The community as a whole turned its back on some schools and would not support them because they were of the opinion that schools did not meet people on equal footing. Many believed that those in charge valued some more than others, and they were right in their thinking because this is exactly what some school administrators did.

It was an unfortunate thing that administrators chose to ignore the school's policies and procedures. They destroyed schools with their flawed thinking and biased decision-making. They didn't seem to realize or perhaps they simply didn't care about the messages they were sending or the implications of their action. If they would not follow school policies, how could they expect students to follow them? Some put themselves above policy and acted as if they were totally exempt from setting good examples and maintaining order. The handbook was there, and the only thing they had to do was use it, but many chose not to. I would not be exaggerating to say that some administrators caused the total decline of their schools.

Many of them acted as if they had no clue of what should or should not take place in a school. One assistant principal's way of dealing with disruptive students was to give them candy. This did not work, of course. They would gobble the sweet treat and return to class with even more energy to carry on and now with a pick at the teacher for turning them in. There was another administrator who would gossip with the students about the teachers. This resulted in teachers opting to keep disruptive students in the classroom as opposed to sending them to this administrator's office. Teachers knew that they would become the villain once the student got to this person's office. This administrator had teachers by the throat. They knew it would be better for them to keep the students in the classroom than send them to the office because what would follow would be his calling them to the office to chastise them and let them know what the students had said about them. This was his way of dealing with undisciplined students, and this only made each situation worse. Students discerned the teachers' reluctance to send them to the office, so their outbursts and disruption escalated. As a result, little to no learning took place in these classrooms. There were very few teachers who would challenge this. Those who did would find themselves on the receiving end of harassment and retaliation. These things might come in the form of extra duty, denial of the most basic necessities such as a request for personal leave. There would be other planned attacks of inconvenience such as changing teachers' schedules, moving them outside the school and putting them in trailers, canceling their extracurricular activities that many worked to supplement their teaching incomes, enticing the parents to attack teachers in bogus conferences where they would attend and side overtly with the parent, regardless of how obviously wrong the parent would be. All of these antics created distrust and bad feelings among the parents, their children, and the teachers. Thus, what was supposed to be a positive learning environment for students became a hard fought battle of wills between teachers and parents perpetrated by administrators; unfortunately, the students would be the real losers. These conditions were created by incompetent, insecure, and vindictive administrators who did not understand the devastating impact of their conduct.

Advice to parents: As aforementioned, be aware of smiling administrators who always wear the face that "all is right with the world." Your concern should be that your child is held accountable for his or her conduct. Know that administrators want the best for their own children and that they would not allow theirs to get away with what they allow yours to get away with. You should want administrators to deal with your child in the same manner and with the same amount of care and concern that they deal with their own. Know too that not all administrators have your child's best interest at heart. Some of them use children to further their own devious causes such as harassing teachers they do not like.

A case in point: One teacher's after-school SAT Prep course was eliminated after she complained about administrators' failure to discipline students. The after-school program was there to benefit the students. Ultimately, they were the ones who missed the opportunity to score high and possibly earn scholarship money. Another teacher lost her job as cheerleading coach because she attempted to discipline a disrespectful cheerleader whose mother happened to be a close friend of the principal.

Acts such as these had an adverse effect on students. Not only did they suffer academically, but their social and emotional growth was hampered by the fact that they were not held accountable for their conduct. The thing that was worse was the message they received about the school and the administrators. Their parents' failure was their inability to see that their children were wrong in most instances, and as a result they did not get to address their children's real issues. And some of them were severe.

Many teachers believed that parents simply did not care enough to get to the real issues and that many of them were willing to overlook their children's behavior as long as they were passing. Their children, however, would be the ones who would suffer in the long run. Take the SAT course, for example. They needed the SAT prep course, not the teacher. They were the ones who would lose out. So, why didn't the parents complain? It was as if academic achievement was not important to them. Many seemed unaware of the kind of power they had or the impact they could make on administrative decisions. They had a voice but wouldn't use it unless their children were disciplined for things such as using a cell phone or violation of dress code. The schools faced many challenges; some greater than others, but many of them were easy fixes. Even so, some administrators chose to look the other way instead of addressing them.

A case in point: One school resource officer seemed to have too casual of a relationship with students. There was always a steady flow of traffic with students walking in and out of his office. It appeared he used his office as a place for social gatherings. Even though some were bothered by it, most teachers would not question this because his office was generally thought to be legitimate, but it also appeared to be another one of those situations where the relationship between the adult and the students was too casual. This situation with the school resource officer was not an isolated incident. A similar incident involved a teacher whose relationship with a female student was questionable. This teacher would neglect his classes to carry on casual conversations with the young lady while his students would basically destroy his classroom. He would spend an entire class period standing outside with this student while the ones inside walked around aimlessly and created chaos.

Incidences like these should not have happened of course, but for unknown reasons, adults in the building were reluctant to speak out. Many looked the other way, and some tolerated the situation. The failure of teachers and administrators to address these kinds of problems only made matters worse, of course.

Advice to Parents: Just simply become involved in your child's life. Know his or her friends, especially their adult friends. Question your child regardless of his or her protests. Do not give in or give up. Many times when children go out of their way to keep parents at a distance, there is a reason for their actions. Do not buy into the notion that your child is just going through that teen phase and is being difficult. There is always the possibility that there are other influences in his or her life. The fact that some of them are willing participants in their own exploitation does not give any adult the right to take advantage of them.

Poor attendance was always an issue and one of the main reasons schools were failures. The teachers couldn't make the students come to school, and this was their legitimate reason for all their failures. Many students failed courses and ultimately failed to graduate because they did not attend school. It was common for some students to miss sixty to seventy days of school without anyone taking the situation seriously. Of course, absenteeism and truancy always took center stage in most faculty meetings, but the issue went unresolved year after year. This, however, did not have to be. There were guidelines and policies in place to decrease absenteeism, but total involvement meant going beyond the school district and involving another county office that had the power to enforce policies and make a real difference. But, it was this office that no one dared to question, and so the issue of truancy persisted for years while young people who were incapable of self-governance were afforded free-will to do as they pleased which involved hanging around their neighborhoods and breaking into peoples' houses while they were at work. In many instances, parents would not know that their children would not be in school. Many would drop them off, and as soon as the parent was out of sight, they would walk off campus. Eventually, the schools developed a system whereby parents would be notified of absences, but in many instances this failed as well because in order for it to work, someone would have to call the parents but this was neglected because there would be so many absences, and the person responsible for calling would be overwhelmed and have to attend to other important things that her job required. The school's failure to address such things created chaos in the community. I recall one of my students telling me that she and her mother hated to leave home because there would always be a group of boys standing on the corner and staring at them as they drove away as if they were waiting for the opportunity to break into their house.

Advice to Parents: Know the offices in your city and county government and the role each plays in working collaboratively with the school system. Hold these people accountable as well. The local school board needs all the help it can get. You can start with your school board's district representative. He or she should be able to set you in the right direction. Most importantly, you should meet regularly with your representatives and voice your concerns. Many of you elect these people and forget about them for the next four years. You take it for granted that your interest will always be theirs. Unfortunately, it does not always work like that. Board members are only people just like you. They can be coerced and manipulated into making decisions that want always be in you or your child's best interest. You must closely monitor their actions. To put it plainly, "You must inspect what you expect." R.S.

The incidences described above were those of a more serious nature. There were others that were not as serious but were quite annoying and could have been corrected without a great deal of effort, but were not. For some sad reason, things seemed to be done in contrast to sound reasoning and just plain common sense. In other words, many actions and decisions defied logic.

Some of these fixes did not require a great deal of thought. Take for example the selection process for prom king and queen. Rather than having students vote for these people on prom night, students voted at school a couple of days before the prom. By the time prom came around, prom king and queen had already been decided, except the announcement was made on the night of the prom. The thing that baffled me about this was that this became a popularity contest. How could students know in advance who would shine at the prom? From all my experiences with proms, the selection of king and queen occurred on the night of because it was a recognition of those individuals (for whatever reason) who stood out. Proms are supposed to be magical. They are a revelation so to speak. They give the shy girl who never gets anything else in the way of recognition a chance to shine. This girl shows up and wows her classmates and ultimately wins the title, Prom Queen. That is the beauty of it all. It's the surprise. But, at our school, it was predetermined. It was a popularity contest. In essence, the same boy and girl who would have won every other contest such as homecoming king and queen would be selected as prom king and queen in advance of prom night. This was unfortunate, especially for the quiet and shy types, those seniors who had not gotten any other recognition that year and who believed that prom (the last big social event of their senior year) would afford them the opportunity to be recognized in a meaningful way. But it did not happen this way because that little bit of hope was extinguished because of the way things were done, and some of them desperately needed this. After all, they weren't the ones their classmates would have ordinarily chosen as senior superlatives, but prom night would have offered just a little hope if it had been done correctly.

A similar situation occurred each year at graduation. Traditionally, there is a valedictorian and a salutatorian. The salutatorian speaks first while the audience eagerly awaits the speech of the valedictorian because it is generally thought to be the highlight of the graduation ceremony. It was the opposite in this school. In was the valedictorian who spoke first. Thus, what was supposed to be the highlight of the graduation ceremony occurred first and then the secondary followed. No one expected the salutatorian's speech to champion the valedictorian's, and usually it did not. I think the confusion had to do with the fact that the valedictorian was called the first honor graduate, and the salutatorian was called the second honor graduate. So those in charge interpreted this to mean that the first honor graduate would speak first and the second honor graduate who was the salutatorian would follow. Even after it was mentioned, those in charge made no attempt to correct this easy fix. This was just one of the many instances when things could have been corrected but were not. This failure to correct these kinds of things had to do with peoples' attitudes toward the one making the suggestion. If they did not like him or her, it did not matter how much sense it made. They simply refused to correct it because they did not want to give that person the satisfaction of being right. They never realized that things of this nature would eventually define our school as poor and low functioning.

Another very disturbing incident happened one day during the changing of classes. When the bell rang, I stepped out into the hallway to see a group of known troublemakers fast approaching; something most definitely was going on, but I was not able to get the full scope until the group reached the area where I was standing. As they passed, I noticed a teacher who was a friend of mine and also one of our new teachers. He was in the middle of the melee. I mouthed to him "What happened?" He mouthed "nothing, nothing, go back;" so that was exactly what I did. I realized he did not want my help even though I was sure he could use it. Regardless, I honored his request. It could have been that he thought my presence would have infuriated the administrators because I had a reputation for calling them out for their negligence when they failed to discipline students, or it could have been that my aggressive nature as a female would highlight his passive flaw as a male. I say flaw because in our school, a passive personality was like the relationship between a cheetah and a gazelle where the teacher would be the gazelle. Someone was going to be the victim and the other the victor. I am sure, however, this teacher would have been able to hold his own under ordinary circumstances, but in our school we were expected to take the high road even when we were abused by the students. Some did and some did not. It was not long after that encounter that I found out what happened. I learned that a boy had walked up on the teacher and attempted to body-slam him. This was especially embarrassing for the entire school because this teacher was young, professional, and smart. He was one of the few that set high standards and reflected the true nature of real educators. He was everything a teacher should be and an excellent role model, especially, for African American males. And for this to happen to him was extremely humiliating for the teachers and the students who really respected and admired him.

Another problem that plagued our school involved homework assignments. One sure way to fail students was to give homework assignments and place a high value on them such as having them count as one-third or one-half of the overall grade. This happened in many classes. Most principals seemed to fear the homework challenge that called for them to recognize and support the fact that not all students were living in conditions that afforded them the opportunity to do homework. We all knew that many of our students lived in deplorable conditions and the opportunities for out-of-class work were non-existent. They didn't have the luxury of doing homework, but principals dreaded that fight and so abandoned it. Most fell in with the status quo and emphasized the importance of teachers assigning homework despite what they knew about students' personal lives. My take on this is that homework has its place, but it should never be the reason a student fails a course because we cannot as educators control what happens after students leave the school. We do not know what happens in their homes. We do not know their lives outside of school. We cannot assume that every child has a nice and neat little personal space where he or she can do homework or if he or she is even living in an environment where something like that is even possible.

My advice to parents is that you are the home-school teachers. Partner with teachers and administrators to plan homework activities and schedules that take into account your unique situation and circumstances. You know that better than anyone else. You know what your child's life is like at home. You know whether or not doing homework is even possible. You know what your child has to contend with at home. You cannot overlook your child's most important needs just to do homework. Even though most educators advocate for homework as an extension of classwork, most would agree that homework should never be an added burden on a struggling family that does not have the luxury of placing a high priority on homework.

Among the many things that went unaddressed, the worst of them all was the nasty black thick slim of what appeared to be mold that crept across the ceiling and flowed down the wall of one teacher's classroom. This was not one of those isolated classrooms hidden out the way from everything else. It was there as plain as day, on the first hall in a highly visible area. I am not suggesting that it would have been alright if this classroom was one of those hidden out of sight. By no means is this my intent. I am saying that it was appalling that school officials ignored this problem when it was in plain sight every day for everyone to see. Now that I look back on it, I am even more shocked that it was unaddressed so long. The teacher and her students met there every day, yet nothing was done. I cannot say for sure it was mold, but it looked very much like it. It was black and thick and always wet, and it seemed to creep down the wall. Regardless of what it was, it should have been dealt with. The appearance alone demanded action.

Irrelevant curriculum also plagued our schools. To teach many of the classics we were required to teach was almost an act of abuse. Many students did not like them and could not relate to them. Time was wasted on literature that was foreign to the students and had no relevance in their lives. Had we focused more on literature that reflected their culture and heritage, we would not have lost so many of them. Unfortunately, many literature textbooks cover only a few works that reflect the lives of African Americans. This devalues and marginalizes African American heritage. Considering the countless works written by blacks for blacks, this should not be the case. Black students should be immersed in the literature of their people instead of the lives of others. Consider the implications of emphasizing the cultures of others while dismissing theirs. Take for example the works of Shakespeare: Personally, I enjoyed his works, but to assume that my students would enjoy them as much was a mistake. I suppose the average Joe on the street has heard of "Romeo and Juliet" but not because it left an indelible mark on him as one of the world's greatest classics, but rather for the hype it sustains in schools even until this day. Somewhere and at some point in our history someone decided that it should be read by every high-school student. But why? Who decided that Shakespeare's works are so great that they simply must be read by every student? Who was so bold in their opinion to make this call for everybody? I am not saying that I did not put my all into teaching it. I did because I like Shakespeare, but many students just simply could not relate to it. It seemed far removed from anything in their lives and I suppose that if it had not been for the effort I put into teaching it, I would have lost many students during the Shakespeare season. Many works like Shakespeare's had little to no relevance for many of the students in our school. Much like the themes that accompany Shakespeare's plays, there was always a common theme that accompanied my teaching of the playwright, and that was "What good is Shakespeare to children who struggle with ordinary English?" This thought permeated my mind. When I attempted to teach Shakespeare, I would have to read the entire play line by line and translate each sentence. By the end of the day, I would be exhausted.

And if having to teach these overrated works was not bad enough, then having to recruit African American students to compete in a one-act play competition whose rules were that the plays performed had to be classics like Shakespeare or others like him, then this was enough to do us in completely. Every year, the schools in the district were expected to compete in the region one-act play competition. The task involved recruiting students and making sure they were academically eligible to compete, meaning that they had to be in good academic standing. This was good, however. The bad involved such things as students having to stay late after school to practice. Many of these children would be exhausted after a long day of attending classes, but they were dedicated, and many of them really enjoyed acting, so they did whatever was necessary, but one thing they would not do was participate in plays that they could not relate to. And no amount of persuasion could keep them coming after school to practice long hours for something they just did not like. I tried so many times to convince them that the rules required a certain kind of play, but this only resulted in them dropping out. Eventually, I had to give in to their wishes if we were going to compete, and I knew they were right in their stance. I do not suppose I should say they were right; "realistic" is a more fitting and appropriate term. These students were simply being themselves. They did not necessarily consider the consequences in their decision to do their own plays, ones that they could identify with. They wanted to be themselves. That was the reason they chose plays like "A Raisin in the Sun," "Mama, I Want to Sing," "Dream Girls," and "My Grandmother Prays for Me." And they performed these plays with precision and pride. Yes, they were something to see, but they never won first or second place. Each year during competition season, they would rehearse unrelentingly. They would stay long hours after school perfecting their skills and making sure they learned every word and every line and with enunciation that would make all their former English teachers brag about having taught them in earlier years. They were great. As time neared for the actual competition, there was only excitement in the air because they were ready. They knew that they had what it would take to win. Their confidence was at an all-time high. So on the day of competition, they drew strong applause, strong calls from the audience, congratulatory hugs and a great deal of hope that all this meant that they stood a chance of winning or at least placing somewhere among the top two, but they never did. After all the plays were performed, the all-white judge panel would retreat to a secluded office somewhere in a building on a predominantly white college campus and emerge about two hours later carrying score sheets, large trophies, and three times as many small ones. Prior to their reentering the auditorium, there would be a great deal of loud talking and laughter and nervous energy as the students and their club sponsors awaited their return. But when they finally reentered the room, a hush would fall over the building, and all eyes would be fixated on them and the shiny trophies they carried as they were proudly placed on the tables that expanded the length of the stage that had seen so much activity that day. Following this, one man would stand and make a statement about competition rules in general. Then he would explain how the winners would be announced. All the while, everyone waited as if they were waiting to hear who had won a fifty-million dollar lottery, but it was a bit more intense than that. So when the time finally came to announce the winners, everything that I knew was confirmed, and everything that my students hoped for was denied them. They had believed that their performance would be enough to secure them a win among the top two. They felt that as long as they performed outstandingly, the type of play would not matter. They felt that a good play was simply that, a good play and that the judges would see this and award them for their performance, but they never did. I, on the other hand, knew and accepted what my students refused to accept. I knew that their performance would be ignored, but I didn't discourage them. I let them reach the zenith. I knew that the all-white judge panel would not select them and that all they wanted was an excuse in the first place and that was that their play was not a classic or what they considered to be a classic. I also knew that they did not even want our students on the stage. I had been schooled by the many comments I had read over the years on the score sheets, such comments as "You used too much of the stage," even when the stage was a small one. I knew what this meant. It meant that some judge was telling us that we had no business even competing; after all, how can actors use too much of the stage? It was a sham and a scam and our children were the victims. In essence, months of rehearsal, staying late after school hungry and exhausted, but dedicated ended with a gigantic slap on the faces of innocent naïve children who were incapable of imaging the level of hatred, jealousy, and resentment that could be directed at them by people they thought would be fair and honest. In this very sad situation, not all was lost however; there was a kind of consolation prize. A case in point, at the end of one of these competitions when the judges were away tallying scores, the white club sponsors jumped on stage and started dancing. They popped and swirled around the stage to the sound of rap and hip hop music that stomped through the high-tech equipment that had been used during competition that day. The music was loud and inviting and in stark contrast to the classical sounds that had been played during performances that day. It was all that students wanted and quite tempting for adults as well. School after school of children and their sponsors took to the stage and even mine ran up and partook of the consolation prize, but when they noticed that some club sponsors were up there dancing the evening away, they ran to the back of the auditorium and grabbed my hand and proceeded to pull on me telling me to come on and join the party and telling me that I was the best dancer of all the sponsors on the stage. They knew that I was a good dancer, for we had danced many a times during some of those explosive rehearsals that brought out the talent in all of us. I would be lying to say that I did not want to take to the stage, for the music was the kind that made you want to move, but I denied myself this opportunity. I knew I could have shown off, but I did not because I also knew that the dance was for us. It was their consolation prize for the Blacks who would not place in the competition after the judges returned to the auditorium to announce the winners. It was, to me, a stereotype that said we could not act, but we could dance. But this was one time that I was not going to give them the satisfaction even if it meant denying myself and my students who I was sure would soon feel the blow just minutes away. And then, I knew what they thought of us. We wouldn't be able to resist the drums and the beat. I knew, as well, that the responsibility of representing our school well was placed squarely on my shoulders at that moment. On that day, I chose to preserve what little dignity we had in this community of bigotry, and from that day until this day, I am glad that I did not fall for the consolation prize. I will always remember and love the students at Monroe Comprehensive High School who participated in the school's Drama Club during my tenure there. I love these people dearly, and the time I spent with them were some of the most beautiful years of my life. I will always remember these students for their tenacity and dedication in the face of adversity and racial discrimination.

My question for parents is when and where did we come to believe and accept that we do not have a voice in what our children are taught and required to learn? Why do we naturally accept others' views of the way things ought to be? As parents, you have the right to say and participate in the process of how things are done. The one-act play competition should never have been designed to ignore the values and interest of African American children. If these things are going on in your schools and communities, challenge them and do not stop until you change them.

The Exceptional Students Program is considered one of the most controversial in many school districts. In one district where I worked, it was the subject of countless complaints. No one really ever seemed to be able to say exactly why this department was dysfunctional, but most everyone acknowledged that it was. While I cannot say for sure, but I suspect it might have had something to do with the fear of lawsuits. Most school administrators seemed reluctant to get at the core of the problem. Instead, they would appoint a special education teacher in the school to deal with special education matters. I'm of the opinion that most did not take it upon themselves to learn the special education laws. They never questioned or challenged anything dealing with special education. They accepted whatever special education people told them. It did not take long for some of these special education people to realize that they could do just about anything because they knew that school administrators would turn a blind eye and deaf ear to any issues dealing with special education. Failure on the part of the administrators to involve themselves in special education issues, caused teachers a great deal of frustration because even though the principals did not seem to understand or care about the issues, many teachers were aware of special education laws. Almost all teachers are required to take a special education (exceptional students) course for certification. They were knowledgeable about the laws and recognized when abuses of the program were at hand. Many complained, but their voices went unheard by reluctant administrators who did not want to challenge special education. In some instances, this created a rift between special education and regular education teachers. Practices of this nature occurred on a regular basis. In addition to this, there were times when the needs of these students were taken for granted. A case in point involved a situation when the school did not have enough standardized tests for every student. When the person in charge of testing realized that many students who would be testing the next day were special needs students, he stated that the test shortage didn't matter because

"They're just special needs student." This attitude toward school in general hampered progress and cheated students out of an education by devaluing them.

One of the worse lapses in judgment and one that directly impacted the students was when the principal on the day of standardized testing decided to use the gym's scoreboard as a time clock. The students were all packed in the gymnasium and ready to test. This was a high stakes test that students had to pass to graduate high school. I was one of the testing coordinators and thought that using a big red scoreboard would be too distracting for the students. Imagine taking a timed-test that you must pass to graduate and having a big red countdown device squarely in your face. The pressure was too great. I suggested that maybe we should use a different device, one less distracting and intimidating. Nothing I said mattered to him/ her because his/her hatred for me was stronger than his/her concern for the students performing well on their tests. He/she was adamant that he/she would use the scoreboard regardless of the impact it might have on test scores. When I realized that this had more to do with me than the students, I went back into the gymnasium to monitor testing. I felt badly about the situation, but he/she was the principal, and there was nothing else I could do. On the next day, he/she called me into his/her office and told me that I could no longer assist with testing. He/she handed me a letter stating the same, but he/she exaggerated the situation by saying that I had been loud in the hallway and created a scene. None of this had happened, of course. He/she simply hated me and took advantage of every opportunity to discredit me. His/her insatiable anger against me did not stop with the letter. Sometimes, during summer break, he/she and a friend principal of his/hers got together and laid out a plan to transfer me. He/she first transferred me to what was considered to be a fairly decent school, and then later, his/her principal friend transferred me to a nontraditional school where someone like myself would have a really difficult time due to my no-nonsense approach to discipline. I will have to say that their plan worked well because that was the last job I had in the district. My contract was not renewed at the end of that school year. I had been put in a situation where I could not win. The principal at the nontraditional school was equally bad as he/she had been, but in my opinion was worse because he/she was biased and didn't seem to care who knew it.

I once heard someone say that hell is the impossibility of reason, meaning that it is a terrible thing to have to deal with those who are unreasonable or are incapable of reasoning or acknowledging the plain and simple truth even when it stares them squarely in the face. Well, I submit to you that I have had to deal with many people in schools who were incapable of reasoning, and it was no joke. When you expected them to use good common sense, their usual reaction was a blank stare, a refusal to acknowledge the plain truth, silence, and an expression that since they were in charge, there was nothing anybody else could do except accept it and live with it. My usual reaction was a feeling of disgust, and fighting the explosion going on in my head. In other words, I just wanted to scream but could not or do anything because they were always looking for a way to make me out to be the bad guy so that I would be the problem and not them with their flawed thinking and failed leadership.

My advice to parents is to take part in every aspect of the daily operations of your child's school. Visit the school prior to major activities such as test preparation and testing. Ask questions about the processes and procedures. Be in the know. Do not take it for granted that educators are always right in their thinking. Remember that they are just people too. Do not be made to feel that you are a troublemaker just because you desire to be involved in your child's school life; but also, as aforementioned, be kind and sincere in your dealings with educators.

Decision-making in the school system was almost always done on the basis of politics and retaliation. Retaliatory acts were quite common. A case in point: A very high-strong coach was accused of cursing at some players. The coach probably had not done this, of course, but it did not matter because the "powers-that-be" wanted him/her gone because he/she was known to speak his/her mind regardless. The real issue was that he/she refused to go along with the politics in the district. Everyone who knew anything about the situation knew that it was the beginning of the end for this coach. So this set-up was a means toward that end. So, the process of elimination began. The coach was falsely accused; the incident was made public by the media; then the coach's job was taken. This was a common act. Your enemies would make a case against you even though it was based on a complete lie. Then, they would expose you in the media, and announce that you have been removed. What was worse was that the school board would never research the accuracy of the false accusations. Many were complaisant and instead of acting as a system of checks and balances, they always went along with the white superintendent who they never realized worked for them. They acted as if he/she was their superior and whatever he/she recommended, they supported. The worse of this was that he/she was bias and unethical and so needed to be monitored. Instead, he/she was left to wreak havoc on the system.

The coach's case was like that of many others. It really did not matter that his/her accusers were lying. Higher-ups considered this a grand opportunity to get rid of this aggressive outspoken person who was a threat to their way of doing things. This was one way that your enemies would get you. They would take what most people already knew about you and blow it out of proportion to make a case against you. Everyone knew this coach was a no-nonsense aggressor on the court and in the classroom as well. Being aggressive and outspoken should not, and in most instances is not considered bad or counterproductive. In fact, most coaches are naturally aggressive; it sort of comes with the job, but unfortunately, aggression is one of those qualities that can be made to seem bad if that is someone's motive. This is exactly the way it was used against the coach. The most unfortunate thing about this was that the students would be the ones who would suffer. They lost a coach who was strong and would stand up for them; a no- nonsense disciplinarian who had connected with generations of families in the community. The kind of person who truly cared and made a positive difference in the lives of students. For many of them, this was the parent they never had. Far more than a teacher and coach, this person was directly involved in their lives. Now, they would be without this strong support system, and even though they signed petitions and appealed to the public via Facebook and other social media, they could not do anything about the actions taken against this person that so many of them had come to love and appreciate. They did what they could but could not make a dent in a system mired in politics and hell bent on retaliation. When I think of the students and the effort they put forth for justice for their coach, I experience a sense of their desperation that reminds me of my own desperate desire to see my deceased mother again in earthly form but knowing all the while that I will not, but still hoping anyway. For these young people, the action taken against their coach was a kind of lost not unlike death. The death of faith in the system, the death of hope, the death of decency and respect, and worst of all, the death of their innocence and belief that truth and honesty trump lies and politics. These students learned what their teachers knew all too well, that being right does not mean anything when you are part of a system that is plagued with dishonesty and run by the good-old-boy network. Deeds like these were quite common.

Another case involved a teacher who was a pivotal part of the school when it came to helping students pass their state-mandated graduation tests. Students needed these tests to graduate from high school, and this teacher made it a personal mission to help them. This teacher was good at this and went above and beyond his/her duties to accomplish this goal. Like the coach, he/she was outspoken and never made apologies for what he/she considered important issues that warranted attention. He/she had come to accept retaliation. After all, he/she had experienced a great deal of it and naturally dreaded it but knew that his/her stance would result in it. But, he/she chose to speak out anyway. As a result, he/she experienced many set-backs.

One of these setbacks was the transfer of the teacher to what was considered the most dreaded school in the system, a school that sent most teachers into immediate retirement or resignation at the simple thought of having to work there. This teacher, however, was strong and was determined not to let the "powers-that-be" run him/her off. He/she weathered the storm of student discipline problems and a principal who was lacking in respect for teachers and students and in his/her abilities to run the school and who demonstrated subtle acts of racism such as suggesting to students that they should not take "welfare", a very antiquated word, or in some instances identifying female students as the ones "with the fake hair." This principal felt especially threatened by this strong outspoken teacher because he/she knew that this person would speak out against apparent improprieties. The principal was overbearing in his/her ways, and his/her conduct created bad blood between him/herself and the teachers, especially in instances where race was a factor. Someone once said that attitude and personality cannot be regulated. Perhaps, they cannot be, but there are strategies that can make them a little less unpleasant and a little easier to deal with. But none of these strategies were ever used in our schools.

There should have been some kind of policy in place that discouraged the principal's description of black girls as the ones with "the fake hair," or policies that discouraged him/her from recognizing whites as "Doctor" while ignoring blacks with doctorate degrees and calling them by their last names without their proper titles. It is a most unfortunate thing that educated people have to be mandated to respect each other, but in some districts it is necessary. The worst thing of all was the thought that if he/she was treating adults this way, he/she was probably treating students much worse behind closed doors.

There were several white administrators who made no attempt to even pretend to be professional in their conduct. It was as if they just devalued the schools and the people in them. There was the guy who would bring his dog to school. I recall going into his office and discovering his dog on the floor under his desk. While I understand people's attachments to their pets, I just believe there's a time and place for any and everything. This was the same person who never really made an attempt to do anything, and this school was on fire with failure. And then there was another who would ask parents out of his office when he could not provide answers to their questions. He would abruptly end a meeting and force parents to present their cases before the school board.

Advice for parents: Teach your children to expect respect and not settle for disrespect. Teach them that when others disrespect them, that this is no reason for them to hang their heads in shame and feel badly about themselves or to blame themselves. More importantly, help them to understand that they must respect themselves if they expect others to respect them. Remind them that this requires a great deal of effort but that its benefits are immeasurable.

Aggressive corrupt principals are bad, but cowardly principals can be worse. Fear impedes growth and brings good things to a standstill.

School is no place for cowardly principals, but unfortunately, many schools are run by them. In fact, some school districts will not hire an administrator unless that person is known to be passive and the kind of person who doesn't question anything but simply follows orders. These people should never be in charge of schools because they are too afraid to ask for the most basic things for their schools. Most choose to suffer in silence than to "make waves" is what they call it. But the sad thing is their misguided thinking that they are making waves if they attempt to secure resources for their schools. Some of them never seem to understand the reason for their jobs as principals __ to act as the school's greatest advocate in academic growth and student achievement, but these things require resources, but unfortunately, many are too afraid to ask. A principal's reluctance to stand up and speak up for his school can be devastating in many ways, and the sad truth is that the students are always the victims.

A case in point: After spending one Sunday at Andersonville National Cemetery watching black men reenact a role as soldiers in the 54th Massachusetts Infantry Regiment during the Civil War, I returned home inspired by what I had seen. My brother had been one of the participants. I quickly came to the conclusion that my students would enjoy such a presentation. While I knew that I could not get the reenactors to come to my school on such short notice, I thought the next best thing would be to get the movie Glory which told the story of these black soldiers, their desire, and ultimate sacrifice in service to their country. I felt this would be very inspirational for our students during Black History month and that they would enjoy seeing it. I planned meticulously for this event, and the students waited in sheer joy as they anticipated the day of the movie, as this was something that rarely happened in my class. The movie would last much longer than a class period so this meant that we would have to spend at least two class periods on two separate days to see all of it. So they relished the thought of watching a movie for two class periods.

The students watched the movie the first day with great anticipation of the second day. But the second day would never happen because at the end of the first day, I was called to the principal's office and was told by him that I could not show the movie. He said that he had been told by the superintendent, who was Caucasian at that time, that teachers could not show that particular movie. I will never know whether he was being truthful or just creating a story out of fear of what the superintendent would do if he found out. Either way, I felt it was a terrible injustice to the students. The movie offered them a great deal of history about their own people and the role they played in American history, and now this knowledge was being withheld from them. And the thing that made it so bad was the fact that the principal, an educated black man, did not have the courage to stand up for the students. These were children he knew well and saw on a daily basis. He knew some personally. Our students were denied many activities and programs that would have benefitted them directly and were of the type that would have boosted their self-esteem and dignity. Unfortunately, fearful administrators were the gate-keepers, and they blocked these programs because they lacked the courage to stand up for teachers and students.

Advice to parents: Take it upon yourselves to teach your children their heritage and history. Do not take it for granted that they will get this in schools. Many educators are afraid to fight for these kinds of things. It is imperative that children know the truth of their heritage. There is a great deal of misinformation and misrepresentation in some textbooks. Challenge these textbooks. Demand the best for your children. Do not sit idly by and do nothing. Do the research and use the most reliable sources. It is imperative that children know who they really are. In order for young people to be able to connect with others and survive in society, they must know from whom and where they came and come to appreciate their ancestors for their diligence, determination, and accomplishments. One month of black history reports where students stand and present the life of a notable black person is not enough.

Progress was hindered in many ways, but the most egregious was that done out of jealousy and bad faith. A case in point was the teacher who wanted to conduct research on the system's unconventional school to determine whether the school was making a real difference for its students. This teacher was working on her doctorate degree and was attempting to do research for her dissertation. Her topic had been approved, and she had been working on certain aspects of the paper for a while. She had come to the point of having to gather data for the study. Hers was a qualitative study so this meant that her data would be interviews or surveys instead of numerical data. Her task would be to pass out surveys to the teachers just to get an idea of their feelings regarding unconventional school programs. It would involve very little time and effort, and it would be simple. But before she could do this, the teacher would have to get permission from the superintendent. She went to him and made her request. The superintendent, however, sent her to the academic support specialist. When she sought permission at this point, she was told that it would not be a good idea to survey teachers because of a pending ethics issue in the system that involved some elementary schools.

To begin with, the issue to which the academic support specialist was referring did not involve any high schools. This teacher would have interviewed only high school teachers. Secondly, the teacher would make her own survey, and she most definitely would not have included any questions that would have put any of the teachers in a compromising position. Her goal was to simply gather some qualitative data to complete her study on the unconventional high-school. Neither this teacher nor her research posed a threat in any way. In fact, she was known as a very mild-mannered and cooperative person; yet, the academic support specialist denied this simple request. The lady never finished her doctoral program. Most importantly, both the unconventional school and the system would have benefitted greatly from such a study, as the system was in a desperate struggle to revamp the school so that its functionality would truly be an option for students who could not function in traditional school settings.

This was unfortunate and not an isolated incident. There were many of this kind in the district. People were denied the simplest requests. It had gotten to the point where people knew in advance they would be denied the most basic requests. It had become common practice to strategize for days about how to succeed in acquiring permission to get or do simple things.

One of the most unfortunate things about this was that many of these things were done out of spite, envy, and the fear by some that others would get ahead of them. In the case of the teacher who sought to survey other teachers, her research was needed. Her study would have provided insight into the effectiveness of the unconventional school programs or at least given school leaders an idea of what was taking place and the attitudes of teachers concerning the programs. But insecure and envious people were the spoilers. They were hampered by their inability to be fair and reasonable and because of this, others suffered; the students in particular.

A note about the academic support specialist who denied the teacher: This person was known to be threatened by the abilities of others. When he/she had been a classroom teacher, under certain school administrators, he/she had been celebrated as being a top-notch teacher, one that was brilliant and set high standards for his/her students. But the truth was that he/she was insecure and threatened by other teachers, especially those who were really effective in teaching and classroom management. He/she, on the other hand, was always given the smartest students and had fewer discipline problems than those teachers who were given the most challenging students. His/her job was a lot less difficult than most. He/she was also celebrated for her knowledge of subject matter, but the truth was that he/she had learned the material verbatim because he/she had taught the same subject for years. It was not like he/she had to figure things out and teach in a way to help the students learn to solve an equation or something of that nature. His/hers was an informational course. After so many years, anyone would have learned it and been able to repeat it. It was parakeet teaching. He/she did not have to think, just recall and repeat.

Even so, he/she had been elevated to the role of academic support specialist by his/her family and friends who worked in the system. He/she, however, was not alone. There were many who had gotten their jobs the same way. And the saddest part of all was the fact that many of these parakeets were in key positions. These were important jobs that warranted the leadership of the best and brightest. Curriculum and academics are major components of any school system. More than any other, they are the reasons for the existence of school itself, but this department was headed by this shallow and envious person who had no experience in this area.

Advice to parents, especially those who have students in unconventional schools: First of all, real unconventional schools are designed to provide the necessary assistance to those students who generally do not do well in a traditional setting. The unconventional school exists to provide the necessary resources and instructions for students in need. The unconventional school in this system, however, was used as a means of punishment. No school should ever be used as punishment. Just think what that says about the school, not to mention the message it sends to the students. I knew one parent, in particular, who agonized over the thought that her son would possibly be sent to the unconventional school because of a childish prank he pulled in middle school. This in itself painted a picture of the nature of the unconventional school in our district. A real unconventional school is welcomed and not feared by parents. When these schools serve their true function, parents are glad to send their children. They see it as a school that will finally address the real needs of their children.

My advice to parents is whenever you are considering whether an unconventional school is the best educational setting for your child, research the programs at the school. Ask school administrators to demonstrate how this setting is in the best interest of your child. Don't just take someone's word for it. Ask for the research and data to support what they say. If you feel that the school is not in the best interest of your child, you do not have to accept it. Ask school administrators for alternatives. Ask them for any assistance they can provide even if it is financial. In many instances, schools are required to assist students financially whenever they cannot or do not offer the services. Some will not tell you this. In at least one district where I worked, teachers were told not to tell parents certain things such as the fact that their child might need to be tested. They didn't want parents to know because the system would have to pay for it. Hopefully, you see the irony in this. The very thing that they should do is the very thing that they try to avoid doing if it's going to cost them. Many school officials never made the connection between their role in assisting students and parents and overall school improvement. In other words, they failed to realize their place and responsibility in assisting parents with the educational needs of their children and how this failure on their part contributed to the failure of their schools.

As much as we like to think that school is a fun place where a lot of productive things happen for children, most of us who really know have to admit that school can be a very uncomfortable setting for some children. There were many sad sights in our schools. As odd as it seemed, many students stood around aimlessly on a regular basis while teachers walked past them without as much as a glance to spur them to move on to class. Many teachers had given up on the most reluctant students and accepted that absolutely nothing could be done to get them to take education seriously. It was not always that the teachers did not care; in some instances, it was rather an acceptance, by some, of the fact that they were powerless in their attempts to get the students to move on to class. Some students had become permanent fixtures in outside corridors and corners. I recall seeing a boy hunched in a corner trying to escape the rain. A teacher asked why he had come to school if all he planned to do was stand in a corner trying to hide from the rain. I remember thinking that this boy's home situation was probably worse than we could imagine. Perhaps, he could not stay home. Maybe his parents kicked him out every day. Perhaps, he could at least get free breakfast and lunch at school. School perhaps, was the only place where he could get just a little bit of attention. Maybe, it was the only time and place where he could see a friend or talk to an adult he liked. While no one knew why this boy had come to school to stand in a corner all day, most accepted it for whatever the reason and chose to forego questions and conclusions. Some actions defied common sense and forced compliance whether we, as teachers, liked it or not.

Some of our school rules were made to be broken, and there were always some teachers who knew when it was necessary to put the interest of the students ahead of the rules. I recall Mrs. Cheryl Bailey (now deceased) who accepted each situation for what it was. In no way was she a negligent teacher. She simply cared more about the students than she did about the rules. On some occasions, I observed her ignore a policy for the sake of a child if she felt the rule was not in the best interest of that student at that particular moment. For instance, if school policy stated "no eating in the classroom," and if a child came to her who appeared hungry, she would not only give him her food or send to the cafeteria for the student but would allow him to eat it right there in the classroom. She loved her students, and they knew it.

I recall it was the last day of school, and my elementary school son wanted to take his MP3 player. I warned him that the teachers were not going to allow him to listen to music even though it was the last day of school. I told him that he would probably get in trouble and that he should leave it home. I repeated to him that there was no teacher in the school who would allow him to listen to his MP3 player. His reply to me was, "Mrs. Roquemore will."

Mrs. Christine Roquemore was a very special teacher and a wonderful human being. She seemed to be blessed with a gift of knowing what was in the best interest of each child, and she tried to give each child what she felt he or she needed. My son was shy and seemed to take pleasure in certain things. Mrs. Roquemore recognized this in him, and tried to allow him those things she felt would make him most comfortable. He grew and became more confident as a result of the things she did for him. That was more than thirty years ago, but I remember it just like it happened yesterday because it was so impacting.

In spite of the many that seem not to care, there are teachers who are genuinely good and truly love students. Parents should not take for granted that they get the kind of support and appreciation they deserve.

When you discover such a teacher as the ones described here, let them know just how much they are appreciated. Just a few days ago, I was planning to call Mrs. Roquemore to thank her for the things she did for my son. I happened to run across another of his teachers and told her how much I appreciated them working with him. I let her know how good it was that I had run into her and told her that I was planning to call Mrs. Roquemmore. She looked at me sadly and told me that Mrs. Roquemore had passed about a month earlier. I felt terribly sad because I had missed another opportunity to tell her what a difference she had made in my child's life.

Some situations did not lend themselves to argument or debate about how we as teachers should respond. A case in point involved a student in my class. I was one who detested sleeping in class. I constantly monitored my classroom to make sure students were not sleeping, and on occasions when I caught one sleeping, I would warn him or her that the consequences would be to stand for a while or go to the principal's office in severe cases. But this incident happened on a day that I will probably never forget. I happened to notice one of my male students sleeping in an almost semi-comatose state. He appeared motionless. I called his name and did not get a response, so I called it several more times. He finally sat up and looked at me. It was then that I asked him why he was sleeping so hard. He looked at me lethargically and told me that he worked until late the night before. And then, he put his head back down on his desk. His actions seemed involuntary and not dependent on my approval or disapproval. I was just at the point when I was about to tell him to sit up when I caught a glimpse of his legs. He was wearing knee-length pants and his legs were so thin and emaciated. They looked so little and pitiful. This image coupled with the expression he had on his face when he had told me that he had worked all night, brought tears to my eyes. He looked so poor and pitiful that my actions were as involuntary as his had been when he laid his head back down on his desk. I immediately stood up and walked straight out the door to the restroom and cried a silent river. I felt so sorry for the boy, and when I returned to the classroom, I could no more ask him to sit up than he could have sat up. This was one time when I allowed sleeping, and perhaps the word "allowed" is not appropriate because I was not a factor in this. There was something deep in him that gave him no say in the matter, and there was something beyond my control that made me accept it. It did not matter that the principal had strict rules against sleeping in class or that teachers would be formally reprimanded if they allowed students to sleep in class. Some months later, a hearing was held for me because the principal had recommended that my contract not be renewed. The principal had not done this because of this incident in particular, but during his testimony, he/she stated that I allowed students to sleep in class. He did this in an attempt to discredit me as a teacher. Knowing what I knew about the situation, I did not offer a rebuttal.

As a teacher, I had to learn to stop blaming students for a thing like sleeping in class. I had to come to understand that this is not always an act of laziness or defiance. It can be more of a surrendering or giving up on everything. Some children cannot do anything else except sleep because schools are forcing on them things that are totally foreign and irrelevant in their lives. Many things they cannot identify with and are powerless to change. Education officials expect these children to be intrinsically motivated and that is why they continue to push this foreign curriculum. The problem is that these children are not naturally motivated. Some of them detest those things that are being forced on them. There are children who have no interest in anything that a school has to offer. The bottom line is that school leaders must come to realize that accommodations for all kinds of children have to be made because trying to motivate those who aren't creates too much stress. What good is it to expend so much time, energy, and frustration on students while destroying teachers? Teachers must survive the process of educating because their lives matter too.

There are several things that could address the needs of the non-motivated. To begin with, no student should be forced to attend school beyond the required legal age if his or her attendance does more harm than good. Students who show up every day and make it impossible for teachers to teach whether they do so intentionally or unintentionally should be redirected into training programs where they can learn a trade or a skill. School leaders should form partnerships with local businesses and companies to provide specialized training for these students and even jobs if possible. For a small amount of money and strict adult supervision, many of these students could learn and gain valuable experience by spending time working in daycare centers, nursing homes, hospitals, factories, and other jobs like these. Opportunities like these would eliminate some of the disciplinary issues teachers have to deal with in the classroom and some of the gangs students join just to have a job and make a little money. Schools can be structured in a way to eliminate some of the problems they face.

Schools can be very complicated when it comes to dealing with students. While you know you want to help as many as you can, you have to be aware of those who will take advantage and abuse your effort and generosities and take you as weak simply because of your loving nature. Something that I saw often used in our school was the tardy scam. It was a way for late students to blame their tardies on teachers. Some of them would hang out in the hall until the very last minute and when they realized they were going to be late for class, they would stop by another teacher's classroom and pretend to have a problem or maybe need an answer to a question. When they would get to their designated class, they would tell their teacher they were detained by another teacher. Usually, the receiving teacher would not question this out of respect for the teacher that supposedly held them and caused them to be late. Few teachers would take the time to find out what really happened. Had they, they would have found out what really transpired. The student would have purposely stopped by the teacher's room and drummed up a conversation just to be able to say later that the teacher held him back. Some teachers were aware of this scam and would not entertain any question or conversation from a student who was supposed to be on his or her way to class. But then, there were some who would fall for anything. And sadly, there were those who just wanted to be liked by the students, and there were some who were afraid of the students, so they let them get away with almost anything.

A case in point: One of our teachers displayed feminine qualities, and he feared the students calling him out for it; therefore, he would not discipline them for fear of their ranting about his feminine tendencies. This was in a very important course that had a state-mandated test that they would have to pass to get their high school diploma. But there was no order. The students were disruptive every day, all day. There was absolutely no control, and consequently, there was little to no teaching done. This teacher, like many others, would only assign lessons that required very little discussion or interaction between his students and himself. This usually resulted in them filling out worksheets or what has now been termed "thinking maps." In actuality, they required very little thinking. Most teachers would select the ones that were very easy and would not generate questions to cut down on the possibility of class disruptions because any attempt to answer a question would generally open the door to a barrage of conversations, none of which would be related to the assignment. They would talk socially and burst into wild laughter and song and create an absolute disaster in the classroom.

Another very tragic aspect of a dysfunctional school environment occurs when those who are in charge never see the big picture. For some unknown reason, many teachers and administrators would sacrifice the students for a special somebody. To make this clearer, let me give some examples of this. There was a teacher who was known to run late for work. He/she was consistently late without a doubt, and everyone knew it. Naturally, some people were outraged by this, but there were many others who were not bothered and some who actually tried to compensate for this teacher's conduct, or perhaps I should say accommodate him/her. For instance, during the time when schedules were being made for teachers, they would assign him/her first period class as his/her planning period so that his/her tardiness would not affect the students. This, of course, was not the proper and professional way to handle this. They were accommodating his/her negligence. He/she would not have another planning period that day. Planning periods are particularly necessary because during this time, teachers are supposed to be preparing their lessons and grading papers to give students immediate feedback not to mention taking care of all the other school-related duties and responsibilities. To accommodate a teacher the way they did this teacher was to take from the students, but many of those who were in charge never seemed to realize that their support of this teacher was actually doing a disservice to his/her students. This was the same teacher who never graded papers and who always gave students passing grades they had not earned.

Nothing works except holding students accountable for grades and conduct. Compromising the school's policies do not work. If they fail they must be given an "F." If they break the rules, they must experience the consequences. Of course, there will be extenuating circumstances, but usually these will be known by others like counselors, and administrators far in advance of grade reporting and the issuing of report cards. School officials should not accept a barrage of excuses created by students at the end of the grading period just so they can go back and do classwork that they should have done during the semester. When administrators and teachers accept this kind of behavior, they create more work and stress for themselves and create a culture of deceptive students who feel they can beat the system at every turn. They never learn to value education because it has come too easily.

People do not seem to appreciate things that they do not esteem. There appears to be something about human nature that makes this true. In order for us to really value something, we must make sacrifices to obtain it. This is evidenced in college preparatory schools and other academic settings where instructors do not just give grades. They make students earn them. Real success comes after a hard fought battle where one struggles and suffers and pull "all –nighters" trying to finish that research paper or solve that difficult equation. Then when one finishes, he appreciates it because it has caused him. He knows what he had to do to get it. This same principle holds true for so many things in life. For example, recall your experience of buying your first car. You worked hard and saved enough money to make the purchase. You did whatever it took to get that car. You wanted it, and you knew that no one was going to get it for you. The ball was in your court, and you had to make a winning shot, and so you did. You worked long hours and any extra time they would give you. You saved for two to three years all the while thinking about a car. Then comes that day when you can go to the dealer and buy it with the cash you have saved. You go in and pick out a car that you can pay for. You sign the paper work, and then you drive off the lot. You will take care of this car because you value it. It costs you many long hours of work and years of savings. No one bought it and handed it to you. You did it on your own. This is the same way it is with schooling. No one values an education that is handed to him and no one rises to low expectations.

Very few students had a healthy fear of teachers and administrators, not to mention school resource officers. Even though they wore a gun and badge, they did not fear them either. Usually, the source of these kinds of reactions or non-reactions results from the messages that people receive. The students never really saw school resource officers as a threat because they were no threat. In many instances, school resource officers would look the other way regardless of the circumstances. For example, when the city passed an ordinance against sagging pants, it did not matter. Students would walk around all day with pants hanging and exposing underwear. School resource officers, however, were oblivious to this. They never cautioned the students, warned them, or anything. Many of them would say that they would do more if the principals allowed them. They blamed the principals for their lack of performance. This all resulted in students' lack of respect for school resource officers. Perhaps, this would not have been so bad if this attitude had been left at school after graduation, but some of these students carried this attitude into the real world which, unlike the schools, was not as lenient and kind.

Some schools were like a kind of bondage. The kind of slavery that many teachers experienced in school was the kind that involved male principals who always wanted a kiss or close hug, but who never wanted to attend to their real needs such as addressing their disciplinary referrals. While they struggled in their classrooms to gain control and do the job they were paid to do, the thing most on their principal's mind was to get close to them. This was not the case with all male principals, but it was the case with some.

In many instances, teachers who were naturally mild-mannered and soft-spoken were labeled incompetent and thus ineffective by administrators, but the real situation was that students would abuse these mild-mannered personalities and sabotage their best efforts to teach. The students would destroy these classes making it impossible for teachers to teach and then run to the gullible principals for refuge and protection after the teacher had written a conduct referral on them. Students knew which teachers the principal did not like or support. Some administrators had made this obvious so when students were referred by those teachers, then, this was just another opportunity for administrators to humiliate them further by either not acting on the disciplinary referral and suggesting that the teacher change his/her strategies, or what was worse, was to put the teacher on a professional development plan which meant that the teacher would be limited to what he or she could do in the classroom. When teachers were put on professional development plans, they could write only so many conduct referrals per day. Regardless of the number of disciplinary issues a teacher might have, he or she could only write no more than three or four per day; in some instances less. So this put teachers in a position to have to ignore several serious disciplinary issues, and needless to say, discipline problems in these classrooms escalated. Another terrible component of these professional development plans was that, in some instances, teachers were required to take classroom management courses during the summer which would take from them their summer vacation time they desperately needed and deserved to spend with their families. All these things happened because administrators did not want to admit nor act upon serious discipline issues in their schools. These kinds of issues went on for years, and even got worse when the state mandated that all of a school's disciplinary infractions be logged in to a state database. As a result of this, some principals became even more desperate in their attempts to hide serious discipline problems in their schools because they feared them be labeled "Dangerous Schools." Here again, this was just another way of concealing the truth about schools. Under these conditions, some schools became so bad that until this day, they are still unmanageable despite the best efforts including billions of dollars used to turn them around.

My advice to parents is to involve yourselves in every aspect of the school, demand better, and hold school officials accountable.

I once attended a women's health fair where officials had cordoned off different sections for blood pressure screenings, BMI, blood glucose, cholesterol, etc. As I took my seat, I noticed that the student intern seemed extremely nervous. She seemed to be having trouble getting her gloves on, and she went through a series of putting them on and taking them off, and then I overheard her telling the nurse that was monitoring her that she was nervous. Before long, she was able to get her gloves on and proceeded to wipe my finger with an alcohol pad all the while shaking. Then she pulled out the little needle and pricked my finger, and when the process was over, I thought to myself how many educators experience this same kind of nervousness when they anticipate teaching students. Educators are just as impacting in people's lives as healthcare providers, but how many of them know this and take their jobs as seriously as these people?

A blatant denial of improprieties, a cover up, a suppression of the truth, retaliation, perpetuating fear; the result was a dilapidated school system that seemingly cannot recover. Many of the system's problems did not have to be. Some problems could have been resolved with a simple acknowledgment of the true causes such as incompetent leadership, unethical and questionable hiring practices and political schemes. The unfortunate thing about all this was that those at the top, the so-called leaders were the main perpetuators of fear. They had their way of sending out a message that if you complained, if you wanted better, if you followed policy and questioned those who did not, then you would be the one who would suffer. This suffering took many forms from being professionally and physically ostracized to a denial of the most basic rights of a teacher. For me personally, it came in the form of nonrenewal of my contract.

After many years of a struggle to save my job and my sanity, I received an official notice via certified mail that my contract would not be renewed for the upcoming school year. I sued the school district and while I did not win the case, I discovered numerous improprieties and unethical practices in doing my research. My lawsuit lasted four years, and it was supported with years of evidence of false accusations against me and unethical conduct committed by some in the district. It would be virtually impossible to outline the years of unethical practices that were directed at me in this document, so I won't do that, however, I will comment on what I perceive to be a flawed system of dealing with dismissals that occur in many school districts.

I discovered that when cases such as mine come before the school board (those who will cast a final vote on whether a teacher will keep or lose his or her job), the board members cast their vote without knowledge of the case. Some school boards use a tribunal (a group of selected individuals, usually retired educators) to hear these cases. The tribunal functions like a jury in a courtroom. They listen and make a determination which is then passed on to the school board. The school board will make a decision on the basis of the tribunal's recommendation. Board members do not involve themselves in the case at all. They don't attend the hearing, and some don't even read the notes or transcript of the hearing. In other words, when they cast their vote on whether a teacher is retained or let go, they have not involved themselves in the situation at all to make a determination as to whether the teacher is being set up, lied on, or being let go because he or she refuses to do the dirty work of over-powering and dishonest administrators. They don't know anything about the case; yet they make a life-changing decision about the teacher. They take his or her career. In a moment, the teacher's life is changed.

Some of them use the excuse that they feel the superintendent has done his or her investigation and research and that they vote up or down without inquiry. But the sad fact is that a superintendent's investigation might not consist of nothing more than a principal making a recommendation not to renew a teacher's contract on the basis of his or her personal feelings and manufactured conflicts to get rid of the teacher. The superintendent him/herself never does any kind of probing or investigating to determine whether allegations against teachers are legitimate. Any names that are put on the school board's agenda becomes the superintendent's recommendation for termination regardless of whether he/she knows the person or the situation. Principals would make a recommendation and shortly thereafter, the teacher's name would appear on the school board's agenda.

The sad fact is that some principals were not held accountable. The school board had conducted itself so carelessly over the years that some principals felt invincible and acted as if they were their own bosses. Not only were teachers transferred, some lost their jobs entirely on the basis of bogus accusations made by vindictive administrators. Some principals operated as if there was no school board. But practices of this nature were common because most decisions were based on a principal's relationship with those who served on the school board, and most of them went out of their way to stay in good with board members. If a principal had a good family friend or fraternity brother or sorority sister on the board, then he or she could get away with almost anything. He or she would not be questioned or even be required to put forth the effort of making his or her claims seem legitimate.

If it is my intent to portray the situation as it was, I have to be honest and portray the situation as it was even though it means exposing myself. There were many times when I was not the professional I should have been or the person who should have been able to do the right thing regardless of whether I thought I was being mistreated. I had very little patience with those who I thought were being deceitful and dishonesty. There were times when I could have taken the high road, but I didn't because I was full of anger. There were days when I went to school intending to be uncooperative and dismissive. I had allowed my anger to control my interactions and reactions. Today, I am a totally different person. When these things were happening to me, the only thing that came to mind was to snap back and to do so fiercely and insultingly. But now I realize that every adverse situation should be an opportunity to change things for the better, to try to understand the other person's point of view, to support him or her even if it doesn't feel right.

To Teachers

You have a moral obligation to speak out and up when you know that students are being cheated out of an education. There should be nothing in a school that is so suppressive and feared that you relinquish your duties and responsibilities to the students. It is more than your job. It is a matter that involves saving lives. You are the parents away from home. You should always practice "in locos parentis." In the absence of parents, you are supposed to step up and do what a parent would for his or her child. These children are left in your care, and you should not take their lives for granted. God has entrusted you with providing for them and loving them to the point where you should want the best for them. If they cannot get this from you, then my question for you is, "Who can they turn to?" You are the ones who work with them on a daily basis. You know more about their academic deficiencies than any other adult, including their parents. You are the ones who provide instructions and then test them. You know each student personally. You know the areas in which they struggle. In most instances, you know why they struggle. You know a great deal about the students you teach. You cannot afford to take your jobs lightly because the alternative is a life of poverty, desperation, and hopelessness for our children as is the case with "My Child." I wonder how much of his condition can be attributed to teachers who failed him. Was there anyone who cared enough to reach out to him to really help him? Was he invisible to teachers? Did he not matter, perhaps, because he looked like he didn't matter? Was it his own conduct that caused teachers to ignore him? Regardless of the circumstances, all children deserve an opportunity of a good education whether they want it or not, and it is the responsibility of the classroom teacher to make it happen in loco parentis.

Resources for Parents and Guardians

Academic Progress Report

Student _____

Teacher _____

Date _____

Course _____

Lesson or Concept	Standards, Goals, Objectives	Student's Grade or Score

Use this form to track your child's progress during the year because he/she will be tested at the end of the year over the standards covered during the school year.

Academic Deficiencies

Terms	Concepts

Many students perform poorly in a course because they enter the course without knowledge of those terms and concepts that are prerequisites. Many courses are progressive, meaning that in order for students to do well, they must know certain concepts going into the course. Many of the math courses fall into this category. Parents should use this form early in the year after teachers have worked with the students long enough to be able to provide this information.

Attendance Report

Teacher or Course	Absences	Tardies

Use this form during the school year to track your child's attendance.

Testing and Other Forms of Assessment

Lesson or Standard Tested	Date	Preparation Tips	Student's Grade or Score

Use this form during the school year to prepare your child for testing.

Standardized Testing Form

Test Type or Course Tested	Date of Testing	Preparation Tips and Tutorials

Use this form to get information on up-coming standardized tests.

Student Disciplinary Action Form

Teacher or Course	Disciplinary Issue or Infraction	Consequences or Action Taken	Person Taking Action

Use this form during the school year and at the end of the school year for your child.

School Climate Form

(Used to track school success and failure)

Disciplinary Action Referrals

Previous Year	Current Year

Standardized Test Results

Test 1	State	County	School
Test 2	State	County	School
Test 3	State	County	School
Test 4	State	County	School
Test 5	State	County	School

Teacher Qualifications

Total Number of Teachers	Number Certified	Number Not Certified

The data should be taken at the end of the school year. The school should be able to provide this information or direct you to those who can.

Academic Vocabulary and Concepts per Subject and/or Grade Level

Grade Level_____ / Course_____

Terms	Concepts

There are specific terms and concepts associated with courses and grade levels. Students tend to perform better when they are familiar with these terms and concepts going into the course. On the elementary level, these terms appear per grade level. Use this form to get these terms and concepts before the upcoming school year. Make sure your child is familiar with these before taking the course or moving on to the next grade level. Schools should be able to provide this information or direct you to those who can.

www.ingramcontent.com/pod-product-compliance
Lightning Source LLC
Chambersburg PA
CBHW032053150426
43194CB00006B/518